Rational Madness

Rational Madness

The Essence of Brand Storytelling

Juuso Kalliala

ıllıBEP

BUSINESS EXPERT PRESS

Leader in applied, concise business books

Rational Madness: The Essence of Brand Storytelling

First published in 2025 by
Business Expert Press, LLC
222 East 46th Street, New York, NY 10017
www.businessexpertpress.com

ISBN-13: 978-1-63742-900-6 (paperback)
ISBN-13: 978-1-63742-901-3 (e-book)

Marketing Collection

First edition: 2025

10 9 8 7 6 5 4 3 2 1

EU SAFETY REPRESENTATIVE
Mare Nostrum Group B.V.
Mauritskade 21D
1091 GC Amsterdam
The Netherlands
gpsr@mare-nostrum.co.uk

Description

Rational Madness: The Essence of Brand Storytelling is a book for marketing professionals who want to bring their brand to the heart of the conversation and to the center of attention. It's for the fearless brand guardians who want people to love their brand and who understand that this also means the brand will have its opponents. And they love that fact.

This book dives into the essence of influence and demonstrates, through concrete examples, that great storytelling is always deeply rooted in psychology and in understanding people's deepest motivations.

Above all, this book is a tribute to creativity and storytelling. Humanity itself is a story, and we live through stories. This book is also more relevant than ever, as carefully crafted narratives are currently shaping the fate of humankind. We rise and fall by the power of narrative. That's why this is not just a book about marketing; it's a book that believes brands can have an impact on the future of humanity.

Contents

List of Figures

Testimonial

"If I were Elliot Hill, CMO of Nike, this is the one book I'd be reading right now. It reignites belief in the power of brand, sharpens the urgency for a stronger narrative, and delivers the concrete ideas for marketers they need to win. Naturally, this would be a good read to the agency people as well."—**Marco Mäkinen, EVP Strategy at TBWA\Helsinki**

Acknowledgments

There's a bunch of people I want to thank—for helping me become a better storyteller and for enabling the creation of this book. When I was studying marketing and creative writing, as my mandatory internship approached, I asked what the best advertising agency in Finland was. That's when I first heard about an agency called hasan & partners. Due to a series of coincidences, I ended up in this legendary advertising agency at the turn of the millennium, where I spent a couple of years as an intern and junior copywriter alongside my studies. I thank my teacher Veli-Antti Aalto for many good teachings, but above all for name-dropping hasan & partners to me. I especially thank Timo Everi, a former shareholder and copywriter at hasan & partners, who initially hired me. From Timo and the now-deceased Petri Pesonen, I learned where the bar for creativity must be set. I learned uncompromising quality and just the kind of madness that is needed in this industry. Thanks also go to the late Ami Hasan, who perhaps brought that rational dimension, which is the other element in brand storytelling. At hasan & partners, I also got to know copywriter Jussi Turhala, whose ability to play with language left a lasting impression on me. I don't think I've ever properly thanked him for giving me so much responsibility right from the start. He led by example, was my mentor, and placed an incredible amount of trust in a twentysomething rookie. So, I thank him now. I deeply respect these legends of the industry, without them, I wouldn't be here. I thank all my work partners with whom I have had the opportunity to grow, sit through long days, curse clueless clients, travel to the ends of the Earth, and celebrate until dawn. If any work partner has taught me to be uncompromising about creativity, he's the brilliant Art Director and designer Miika Kumpulainen, with whom I burned the midnight lamp more than with anyone else during my years in the advertising agencies. Many thanks to Jukka Hakala, you were the first to hear about this project, which I foolishly blurted out over lunch before I had written a single word. Unknowingly, you were a significant motivator: If someone knows about this project, I cannot leave it unfinished! You were also the first to read the earliest version of the manuscript. Your comments and insights were truly valuable, and they helped the book take its final shape. Marco Mäkinen, it's a privilege to know you. The fact that you read 300 business books a year makes you an undisputed specialist in this field. I've naturally been excited about this book, but your unwavering support and recognition of its potential (after reading it not just once, but twice) have been invaluable to me.

This book was, for a long time, just a strange project that helped me dream and sometimes simply served as escapism. At some point, however, it was time to see what kind of reception the manuscript would receive in the world. Writing careful cover letters and finding potential contacts was at times a painful process. That's why I will forever remember how Scott Isenberg from Business Expert Press (BEP) Publishing responded to my e-mail—quite quickly, in fact—and showed his interest. He has been incredibly open and encouraging, and without him, *Rational Madness* might never have seen the light of day. So, thank you, Scott, and the entire professional team at BEP Publishing! Thank you also to my current employer, S Group, and my closest colleague Lauri Toivonen for allowing me to be part of Finland's most ambitious marketing organization. I have a view of the brightest pinnacle of the industry and the support to improve myself as a brand storyteller every day. As I mention in the book, Teppo Hulkkonen, who has created both illustrations and other graphic elements for this book, is an incredibly smooth and skilled professional!

In a completely critical role for enabling the birth of this book is my wife Maiju, who has ensured the peace for writing amid these busy years. You have supported, encouraged, and been patient. With a backbone like you in life, nothing is impossible.

PART 1

Introduction: The Backstory of the Story

This book serves as a good example of how there's always a seed of something new and positive in a crisis. When the coronavirus caused a pandemic in the spring of 2020, I was, to put it bluntly, in a bit of a tight spot. In the fall of 2019, I had decided to break away from more stable advertising agency relationships where I had worked as a freelancer for almost 20 years and rely more on my own business. My transitional plan was to occasionally take freelance cases, but mainly focus on the creative consultant role where I could help brands directly. However, by March 2020, the situation was such that the pandemic and the subsequent apocalyptic mood froze the highly economic vulnerable advertising industry—and freelance work especially came to a standstill. In this situation, I had to completely rethink my plans. I had envisioned becoming a creative consultant in the future, capable of bringing fresh thinking to big advertisers concerning marketing and brand storytelling. With no real job opportunities and people forced to stay at home, I decided to live in my imaginary world for a moment and build creative concepts for existing brands as thought exercises. When ideas started to flow and I wrote them down, I realized how exhilarating it was. I was free from the constraints of everyday life and from the rationalism, compromises, and deeply rooted lack of courage that often disrupt genuine creative work in marketing communications, even though even in basic marketing courses it should be clear to everyone that creating mediocre or nondescript marketing communications is the most expensive form of communication. Or, to put it more bluntly, it's mostly a waste of money. Competent marketing management should demand sharper, more relevant initiatives from their marketing departments. Where are the social media hullabaloos?

Where are the crowds defending the brand, and where are the passionate opponents?

While working on these ideas, I also started to develop a way to evaluate the strengths of marketing communications concepts. I pondered how creative concepts should be presented and justified. Too often in my work, I have witnessed presentations where the advertising agency has come up with a creative idea without a truly deep understanding of either the core of the brand or what really moves people from a psychological perspective. The latter, especially, began to fascinate me. When you examine all iconic marketing communication concepts, you can see that they always have a deep psychological dimension. On the other hand, also what I particularly like in my work, a good creative process, always, not only involves a rational understanding of the brand, the market, and people but also diving headfirst into the unknown based on complete intuition. This is where the name of my book came from. This dualistic and even paradoxical aspect of this field is precisely the element that has kept me intrigued from one decade to another. This schizophrenic element has also caused more gray hairs than my colicky first-born—and overall makes the industry such that it is not suitable for everyone. But for those whom it is, it offers something that no other field offers.

The world is full of marketing books. That's why the threshold for writing a new one was especially high for me. But I noticed a factor that made me embark on this project: The marketing books I've read are mainly based on theory—and looking backward and analyzing cases that have already been done, as well as telling good and enlightening war stories. I decided to try and see things from a new perspective. What if I could shed light on my thoughts with concrete examples? Examples that would help in understanding my viewpoint that a good marketer must, to some extent, understand human psychology, underlying motives, and needs—as well as demonstrate the power of creativity and storytelling. I found the thought particularly liberating that within the framework of the book, I could use my creativity completely unrestrainedly and exemplify my thinking through the world's most famous brands. Since the primary goal of my book is not to be a sales presentation, it was therapeutic to just let go. I also fully understand that the daily life of brands is often considerably complex, and I can't guess all the individual challenges or business cases that a brand tries to solve. On the other hand, the day-to-day life of marketing departments often falls apart into seeking small short-term partial victories, and we forget to think big. Think in a way that aims for the brand's product or service to become more desirable than competitors for some deeper reason other than just price or product features. Why this matter? It's important, because when a competitor enters the market with a cheaper price or better features, the brand immediately faces problems. There's no loyalty because there's no emotional bond between the brand and its audience.

So, I dove into my own parallel reality and began living life as a brand storyteller without the burdens of real life. And I really went for it with gusto.

I also wanted to bring an element into the book that is usually missing from marketing books but is an essential part of presenting creative work in the worlds of movies, games, and marketing alike: a storyboard or some other visual way to illustrate a creative idea. I thought that illustrations would bring a new airy element to the book, breaking the mold of traditional marketing books. I am extremely grateful that Teppo Hulkkonen joined this project. His illustrations are just a great add!

And as one might expect, by introducing new creative ideas, one also inevitably exposes oneself to ruthless criticism. But that is the core of my whole philosophy: If everyone agreed with the creative ideas in this book, they would not be exceptional enough. Thank you already at this stage for picking up this book—wishing you an enjoyable reading experience!

CHAPTER 1

Storytelling as a Weapon

Storytelling is an ancient way to influence the human mind and human behavior. Through stories, heroes, enemies, and cultural heritage have been created, and storytelling has also been used for educational purposes. Storytelling is thousands of years older than the concept of branding, but if we think about what branding really is—reputation and perceptions—those elements have certainly existed in commerce long before anyone knew how to use them systematically the way we understand marketing today. Imagine a situation where some members of an ancient village went fishing every day and then bartered their catch for goods produced by others. I am absolutely certain that some fishermen were able to trade their catch more easily than others. Was it because they were somehow more likable personalities? Perhaps they told great and entertaining stories during the trade? Maybe they had a reputation as fishermen who could keep their fish fresher than others? It was about brand, reputation, and storytelling. About emotions that guided human behavior and made people prefer one supplier, in this case, a fisherman, over another.

Today, marketing is a sophisticated and analytical practice, almost a science—certainly one requiring solid expertise. But at its core, it is still about reputation and perceptions. In that sense, nothing has changed since the dawn of humankind. As human beings we are driven by both reason and emotion, but emotion is by far the stronger motivator. Yet ironically, as marketing becomes more analytical, truly iconic, intuitively powerful brand stories have become rarer. Why? Perhaps too much theory is paralyzing the creative process. Perhaps, in our quest for rationality, we are forgetting the irreplaceable value of intuition. Did the creative agency's idea make you laugh spontaneously before you started analyzing it? If not, it wasn't a good idea—at least not if humor is at the core of the brand. I have been in too many meetings where people try to rationalize a creative idea into something better, even though the intuitive first reaction was already lukewarm.

In any case, storytelling is the final stage of the marketing process where all the strategic choices are condensed into something that should captivate the brand's audience. Storytelling is the part of marketing that ignites my passion, because I feel like I am part of an unbroken continuum stretching back to the earliest days of humankind—a continuum where Odysseus rides into the Trojan War with the Old Spice man at its side—and I have a seat just behind the saddle.

CHAPTER 2

The Business of Renaissance People

I have noticed that the best professionals in this business can be seen as sort of Renaissance people. They are not professor-level specialists in one particular thing but are interested in a broad range of subjects—and most importantly, they combine analytical and intuitive aspects in a fruitful way. At the same time, it is painful to see people in the industry who are dominated by one side or the other. Pure analytical thinking easily leads to routine, formulaic performances that, at best, are just slightly above mediocre. And then, on the other hand, it's particularly annoying to encounter someone who throws out creative ideas without understanding the core of the brand, and is not interested in business cases and the mental landscape of the target audience. Nevertheless, I want to advocate for advertisers to deeply understand the following fact: In the end, it doesn't really matter what the marketing strategy slides in PowerPoint say. The only thing that matters is actions. Marketing is always something concrete; actions that people can sense, experience, and evaluate. That's why my general advice and motto for advertisers is this: Of course, understand your brand and your target audience, but focus above all on producing as legendary marketing ideas as possible—and invest your last dime to produce those ideas with the highest quality possible. A good brand is like that person at cocktail parties around whom a circle of people always gathers, laughing their ass off. Be the brand that people want to go to the after-party with as well.

I've also pondered the mindset of people on the advertiser's side. I firmly believe that a marketer can approach their work in two ways: one, where they use creative storytelling to achieve sales and branding goals. The brand evolves in the desired direction and the sales team is satisfied. These professionals account for 99 percent of marketing people. And at this point, it's good to emphasize that many of them do their job excellently. They prioritize the brand and the company, and there's nothing wrong with that. On the contrary, that's how a professional should surely think. And then there's that one percent who see things a little differently. But this difference is dramatic. The crucial difference in perspective relates to the fact that most people would like to achieve something big in their life and leave their mark in history somehow. Just ask yourself: Would I like my marketing feats to be written about in university textbooks? Would I like the campaign or brand concept I created to truly become a news topic? To force decision makers in government level to react, to take a position? To divide people for and against? However, few are actually so ambitious, audacious, fearless, and selfish to genuinely aim for a place among the immortals. In the marketing industry, this one percent mindset manifests in a way that the individual uses the field to achieve something that satisfies their own ego. It sounds outrageous, but the good side of it is that these people and their achievements are usually also commercial success stories, and therefore invaluable to brands. Marketing actions striving for legendary status not only meet sales targets, but they also blow them up. At best, a big enough brand action or story can be a generational experience and change the way thousands of people think and see the world—and engage people with the brand at a nearly fanatical level.

I have also used an analogy that fairly well describes these two mindsets. I believe that this same dichotomy was visible at the dawn of human history. There were those who stated that there was plenty of small game near the tribe: squirrels, rabbits, and whatnot—easily caught with relatively little effort and practically no risk. The only downside was that you had to hunt diligently every day—and hardly any stories were told about these hunting trips around the campfire, nor were sagas created that would pass from generation to generation. Then there was the other group that set out audaciously to catch mammoths or whatever large game happened to be living nearby. These animals might have been tens of kilometers away, and upon encountering, the hunt itself would become a life-or-death struggle where almost certainly some of the hunting party got injured, some even paradoxically paid for the pursuit of immortality with their lives. Why go to this trouble and put yourself at risk? Rationally, of course, it's likely because a successful hunt would feed the tribe for months, but I don't believe for a moment that was the only motivator. A heroic act has intrinsic value. It automatically puts its performer in the spotlight, an object of admiration, the main role in campfire stories. And the same motivator drives the marketing person to present in the company's corner office an utterly grandiose idea that will certainly raise a social media storm, boycotts, or political grumblings—but on the other hand, unprecedented fandom. Because that mammoth just has to be taken down.

We are seeing 4,000 to 10,000 commercial messages a day—and to be honest most of them are utterly meaningless crap. On the other hand, this enormous amount of messaging inevitably has a massive impact on us, whether we like it or not. Since the number of messages we see daily is so vast, there's also a significant power of change within it. If even a portion of these messages were harnessed to reinforce brand values in some meaningful and interesting way, people's attitudes could change overall, but a bigger question haunts my mind: Could brands also be shaping the world into something different, perhaps better? With these thoughts in mind, I began writing this book. And in the few years during the writing process, the world has also changed in such a way that I feel the weight of my thoughts has only grown. The world is heading in a more chaotic direction; the growth of polarization, which was already at a worrying level when I started this book, has only continued to increase. The world is full of conflicts and now wars are also being fought in Europe. The world's largest powers are rattling their sabers and openly talking about a new multipolarity of power, where democratic values are threatened. People are experiencing existential angst, uncertainty, and even fear. People have more and more options and choices, but the feelings of insignificance and powerlessness regarding the control of their own lives only increase. At this moment, brands have an exceptional opportunity to find increasingly meaningful answers to the Simon Sinek's brilliant question: Why do they exist?

I wanted to write a book that would be inspiring and see opportunities in this time. I wanted to show with practical examples that brands can genuinely change the way people think, grow as individuals, and see themselves as part of this world—and even offer the opportunity to simply laugh at the phenomena of our time and find absurd comfort in a brand when the world turns upside down around them. And through all this, I want to demonstrate, with solid reasoning, that my thinking also carries significant business potential.

CHAPTER 3

The Fundaments of Brand Building

Timeless topic: what is a brand? There are a thousand different definitions—here's my two cents. A brand is a commercial feature that supports your ego. A brand represents values that you can—and want to—identify with. In other words, a brand cannot exist unless it stands for something that a sufficiently large commercial target audience feel is their own. That's why a strong brand concept must always be based on a human insight, sometimes even unconsciously. This doesn't mean that marketing communications should be the work of psychologists, but based on my own experience, it suffices to be interested in the movements of the human mind at a mundane level and to understand basic mechanisms of human behavior. It's easy to analyze existing cases—and that's exactly why I want to focus in this book on generating new creative ideas and exemplifying my perspective to brand storytelling. However, a few analyses of existing marketing communication concepts can be allowed in this introduction. When speaking about the psychological dimension, I find myself repeatedly returning to Nike and its marketing communication concept "Just Do It." It is, in my opinion, a brilliant example. Its psychological insight and therefore strength is based, at least according to my own analysis, on the fact that humans have been accustomed for a hundred thousand years to be economical in terms of their own energy consumption. Humans have moved practically only when compelled to do so and rested whenever possible. In developed societies, this has caused a massive problem as food is abundantly available and there are no natural reasons to move anymore. For most people, moving just for the sake of moving is a significant mental effort—even though, fortunately, our body has built an endorphin pump that ultimately rewards the mover. Nike's idea that you are your own biggest competitor or opponent is an excellent creative insight. It's easily recognizable in each of our everyday lives and contains a profound truth about human behavioral mechanisms. So, the basis for Nike's brand existence is rooted in strong psychological insight, whether it was a conscious choice or not. This psychological aspect has started to fascinate me more and more, because even after making this observation, I've been paying particular attention to how fragile the foundation is for many creative outputs that are today claimed to be brand concepts. And perhaps a small clarification is in order here: A brand concept should ideally be created only once in a brand's history—or at least with the ambition that it will last for decades. Sometimes the brand concept and a campaign concept get confused, and a single campaign—lasting maybe just a week or two—ends up becoming an overloaded "monster" where every possible expectation is crammed into it. Simply put, when a brand team takes the time to properly develop a brand concept, it can solve the brand's core challenge for years and save an enormous amount of time and energy later during individual campaign planning. In this book, my focus is specifically on brand concepts. I illustrate them with individual dramatizations only to ensure that the ideas don't remain purely theoretical or high-level abstractions.

Basically, there are two kinds of marketing: one that aims for short-term sales and the other that may not aim for immediate sales but wants to establish the values that the brand stands for. I find myself surprisingly often having to explain the significance of the latter. When I entered the industry, the late founder and CEO of the advertising agency hasan & partners, Ami Hasan, sat a then twentysomething novice at the head of the table and explained in two sentences what brand building or this entire field is about: The task of marketing communication is to build an emotional bond between the brand and its target group. People reward this emotional bond with purchase loyalty and a willingness to pay a higher price for the product or service. That's it. Those two sentences were burned into the young creative's consciousness in flaming letters, and they are still the core truth of all my marketing communication. Another adage permanently etched in my mind was printed in giant letters on the wall of the advertising agency DDB Helsinki, and the quote belongs to none other than Bill Bernbach himself: "If you stand for something, you will always find some people for you and some people against you. If you stand for nothing, you will find nobody against you, and nobody for you."

Bernbach's idea is fascinating. Brands need to stand for something. They need to make statements. Have values and opinions. I see that the task of marketing concepts is precisely to find a perspective on this world that allows making statements in a way that is relevant to the brand and its audience. Dramatizing just the product features without a concept can create shooting stars, even delightful insights, but never a systematic approach that would generate a clear brand image for years to come. Yet every creative process must end with seeking that one, most brilliant dramatization. Because a good concept is only the foundation; dramatizations secure the brand's place in people's hearts. Sometimes marketing communication can successfully combine both the underlying big brand concept and the concrete product features. The example that comes to mind is the Burger King's concept which leans strongly just one feature: their burgers are flame grilled. But as we have seen, Burger King's sales and market share haven't developed very well. Could one reason be that the brand concept is based on a feature rather than a value? Quite often though, there really is no concrete feature to communicate, and it could be a blessing. To be honest, there is nothing overwhelmingly superior in Nike and Adidas shoes compared to their competitors. The real differences between grocery stores are marginal from the consumer's point of view; the same applies for lager beers, insurance products, and countless other industries and their hundreds of brands. So, how do these brands manage to be meaningful to consumers? Simply through marketing, marketing communications, and brand storytelling.

When discussing marketing communication, the role of an individual advertisement can be direct selling. *However, the ultimate task of marketing is to make the brand so desirable that people prefer it over competing brands.* So, when speaking of long-term marketing, we are selling the brand, not any specific product or service. Anyone—and I want to emphasize this—anyone can create an ad whose sole purpose is to sell a product or service in the short term. Product and price. Boom, job done. Of course, even that can be done better or worse, like everything else in life. But very few can do marketing that makes the brand more desirable than competitors in the long run. Marketing that rises above all the noise in the media with a clear, understandable, exceptional, and appealing message is really hard to do. And yes, I fully understand that a brand needs both brand building and performance marketing, but since only one of them requires deep understanding of humanity and emotions building, that's the part I'm focusing on. Mark Ritson has described the situation brilliantly: Brand building (long-term marketing) generates brand equity, whereas performance marketing (short-term) exploits that brand equity. It perfectly illustrates the relationship and hierarchy between these two types of marketing efforts.

Marketing is a fascinating industry. I'm not sure if any other area of business has had as many books written about it, and yet, after more than 20 years in the industry, I can say from personal experience that only a few core aspects of marketing have truly changed. Still, books overflowing with marketing theory keep appearing like mushrooms after the rain—relentlessly. If you want to hear everything essential about the fundamental principles of marketing, listen to Mark Ritson. He has said all that needs to be said, and in almost every case, he is right.

But what I find most interesting about marketing—and especially marketing communications—is that it always ultimately comes down to something concrete. And therein lies the paradox of this industry: it attracts an endless stream of theorists who flood LinkedIn feeds with their insights and wise theories. Yes, a brand needs both long-term and short-term activities. Yes, without long-term efforts, a brand cannot build emotional engagement with people. Yes, a single advertisement should convey only one message—cramming multiple messages into an ad will diminish the impact of all of them. This is why, in principle, short-term marketing should be branded only with a logo—because an emotional brand concept message combined with a tactical message already constitutes two messages. This assumes that the audience already associates a value, attitude, or emotion with the logo, which has been built through long-term marketing efforts. Phew, should I turn this into a visual graph? Maybe I should. Should I use Nike as an example? Maybe I should. And I promise, there will not be too many graphs. But here's one, nonetheless (Figure 1).

And even though I occasionally slip into theorizing while writing this book, at the end of the day, this is a business for doers. Only the tangible outcome matters. Who is more respected: the one who theoretically

THE MESSAGING SYSTEM

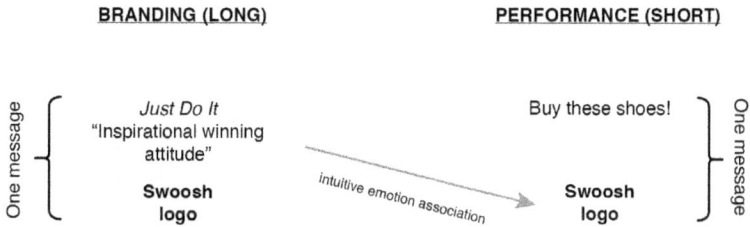

BRANDING (LONG)   PERFORMANCE (SHORT)

One message

Just Do It
"Inspirational winning
attitude"

**Swoosh
logo**

intuitive emotion association →

Buy these shoes!

**Swoosh
logo**

One message

Figure 1 The Messaging System

knows how to forge a samurai sword or the one who has mastered the craft and can create a truly unique blade?

And when I talk about doers, I don't just mean creative designers, graphic artists, production companies, or film directors. This business also belongs to those who can think in new ways, make strategic moves, and position a brand in a truly unique way. The unifying factor in a brilliant marketing team is innovative thinking—something that extends across the entire team.

CHAPTER 4

The Human Shield of an Idea

When a psychologically strong approach has been found and it has crystallized into a unique marketing concept, the purgatory of the person responsible for the brand's distinctiveness begins. A clear vision is like a juicy carcass in the middle of a desert. It is approached by thousands of different parties from ants to hyenas, intending to benefit as much as possible from this delicacy. The clear brand marketing concept is nibbled at by thousands of different parties, and there is a great danger that these nibblers will consume the brand's understandable and articulate position in this world. The sales department thinks that marketing has once again invented some nonsense, which doesn't really matter if it sells these sneakers, nuts, or milk—preferably tomorrow. Some media guy will come and say that's nice, but no one in our channel consumes content for more than two seconds. A brain researcher will tell you that, scientifically, smiling people and possibly puppies are the best way to convey the brand's message. Just make sure nothing negative is shown. I salute those professionals who, in this maelstrom, can hold on to that original bright idea and still get something sensible on the air. I have noticed in my work that creating a new creative concept can be an extremely laborious process, but it is at least as critical to act as the protector, shield, and even front fighter of that bright core idea. And now that it came to mind, I want to point out one more thing about negativity and brain imaging studies. I've argued with an expert from a research institute about the assumption that if a study shows content triggering a fight-or-flight response in the viewer, it's always catastrophic for business. Alright then, but do you know what is the fourth profitable genre in Hollywood? Horror! People are willing to pay to experience feelings of fear—what neuroscientists call the fight-or-flight response, just like they are willing to pay a premium for a beverage called Liquid Death. And one more example from a slightly different angle: what human driver makes people want to ride the scariest attractions in amusement parks? Isn't the feeling you get on a completely insane roller coaster or in a haunted house essentially a pure fight-or-flight response—one that people are more than willing to pay a hefty sum for? We are much more complex creatures than one might initially think. And don't get me wrong—I fully understand the aim of eye-tracking and brain imaging studies. The big misunderstanding happens when people fail to grasp what marketing is actually trying to achieve in each case. It's probably somewhat true that, for example, a smiling person triggers some kind of positive reaction deep in the reptilian brain. But that only matters in certain marketing contexts—mostly, in my opinion, in short-term sales-driven actions. In that scenario, yes, a smiling person trying to sell you toothpaste is probably more effective for sales than someone crying or looking angry. Makes sense.

But when we're talking about a brand concept, I want to talk about what makes a brand famous. And let me tell you—a smiling person doesn't do that alone. But Apple's "1984" commercial did. And you can be sure that the imagery in that ad was far more about triggering the fight-or-flight response than stimulating the brain's pleasure centers. All in all—protect big ideas, break formulas and conventions, and make people feel something, deeply.

CHAPTER 5

The Channel Is a Servant, Not a Master

Digital channels have gobbled up a large portion of brand budgets, and why wouldn't they? Digital channels can easily reach large audiences and target messages to a very specific group. However, when it comes to building emotional connections, digital channels cannot be talked about as a single entity. There are significant differences in how content is consumed across various channels. I won't be looping on this very long, but what I want to say is that you can't tell a story that builds an emotional connection in a channel where the consumer's way of consuming content gives the brand less than two seconds to tell its story. A clear creative thought or idea is, of course, somewhat channel-agnostic. But there used to be a concept called the elevator pitch, meaning that the sales pitch had to be delivered during an elevator ride. That forced a focus on the essentials. But not in two seconds. No one can do that. Our way of telling and listening to stories has evolved over thousands of years. The best storytellers can build tension, perhaps mislead—and then free the audience after an exhilarating, amusing, or terrifying conclusion to continue their lives sometimes as changed individuals. I promise to immediately change my mind and retract my statements the day Hollywood produces a blockbuster movie that lasts two seconds.

Fortunately, we also have excellent digital channels that are great for even longer storytelling formats. But whatever channel you choose, the channel is not the solution for captivating the audience; the content is. So only create stories that respect your audience by striving to be as interesting as possible. And better save your money if you have nothing genuinely interesting to say.

Perhaps slightly off topic, but this is a good moment to highlight another perspective on how strong storytelling also has commercial impact—and how modern marketers should view the potential of story-telling. In 2004, the hit film *Sideways* was released, set in California and charmingly weaving local wines into the plot. The story celebrated wines made from Pinot Noir grapes, while Merlot was disliked by one of the main characters for personal reasons. From 2005 to 2008, global sales of Merlot wines dropped by 2%, while Pinot Noir sales grew by 16%! The film also boosted tourism in the wine regions where it was set. Another example: the economic impact of the Harry Potter books and films on tourism in England—and especially in London—has been in the billions. If Harry Potter had been a marketing initiative by London's tourism office, it would be unparalleled. Just like *Sideways* could have been a marketing masterpiece of Californian wine producers.

As the media landscape fragments, the fundamentals of good storytelling remain unchanged—people love stories. But brands could be much bolder in creating content ecosystems that audiences might even be willing to pay for, no matter of the channel.

CHAPTER 6

Strong Brands Are Elastic

Simon Sinek aptly said that companies need to ask themselves why they exist. I won't argue against that; it's an essential question, but to me it's a matter of perspective. Companies exist solely because they meet human needs. If a company does not fulfill some basic human need, it has no chance of success. And here, I'm specifically talking from the perspective of brands. Apple understood that people want a simpler world, not a more complicated one. In the computer industry, there was a status quo dominated by the hegemony of engineering-driven technological religion. There was a need and demand for a revolutionary message—and into that fertile ground, Apple's message has cut through like a hot knife through butter. But one can't be revolutionary without a counterforce to challenge, an audience that is fed up with the existing situation, and a psychological cornerstone upon which to build.

Human basic needs are age-old, but new needs also arise. For example, the need for environmental protection stems to some extent from the need for survival, but a similar collective need has not appeared in humanity before the birth of the environmental movement in the 1970s. Therefore, brands like Patagonia have evolved from being mountain climbing clothing makers to activist brands that, for example, direct a percentage of their revenue to environmental protection. Patagonia is a good example of an elastic brand whose original idea was not necessarily to increase environmental awareness or act particularly responsibly but to quite naturally change their core brand and basic philosophy as a clothing brand for people who move in nature—and value the nature. The brand can find its brand philosophy and can easily grow toward responsibility and even environmental activism, as the world changes around the brand and the deteriorating state of the environment has come into the consciousness of enough people. What I want to say is that brands should have something meaningful to say. And I want to immediately correct one possible misconception: Meaningful for the recipient can also be, for example, not taking the world too seriously. For instance, Skittles has ended up with a completely crazy brand personality, which I believe resonates with recipients precisely because our world has in many ways become more serious, and there's clearly a need for a counterforce. In these times, the strength of a brand like Skittles is simply to find absurdity in the world and make the most of it. When this kind of thinking is deeply embedded in the brand's DNA and the brand systematically implements this core—and when the message has resonance in people's minds—the brand can create a long-lasting, distinctive, and even iconic relationship with people. Like Skittles has chosen, the humor might be a strong brand asset. Humor often relies on a new perspective on this world or a surprising discovery, so often good humor also appeals to our intellectual side. And when a brand behaves in a humorous manner, the magic dust of wittiness also falls on people who buy the brand's products or services. A simple and effective psychological mechanism that has been tested thousands of times. But if humor or intelligence is just a one-dimensional behavior for the sake of behavior, no matter how smart, I would argue that it's not a very long-lasting choice. In my opinion, this kind of approach to marketing communication is its own genre altogether. Often the aim is simply to tell a joke that's as funny and entertaining as possible, sometimes even one that's so good that it could be seen during a Super Bowl commercial break. And I have nothing against it. At best, these are intuitively entertaining and rewarding individual or at most campaignlike brand acts that leave an excellent memory trace for the recipient. But in this book, I aim to go to a somewhat deeper and more conceptual level.

CHAPTER 7

Modern Marketer and Content Responsibility

I came across a study stating that only six percent of all marketing communications are impactful. This is a dramatic and depressing figure. The majority of commercial messages we see—or don't even notice—are meaningless noise. Late WARC (World Advertising Research Center) research shows that the percentage of unnoticed advertising is almost 90 percent! This brings me to the topic of responsibility, which has been a hot topic for all companies in recent years. It has also been evident in Cannes, where an increasing number of award-winning ads or campaigns are related to responsibility, sustainability, and so on. But I have a different perspective on this subject.

When examining the carbon footprint of digital marketing, it quickly becomes apparent that it has a massive environmental impact. In 2023, the entire Internet's carbon footprint was as large as that of the entire aviation industry, and it's predicted to double by 2025. I'd call that astonishingly exponential growth. I also came across a calculation showing that in the UK, the average digital campaign featuring a single video generates as much greenhouse gas emissions as three round-trip flights between Paris and New York. And this figure only accounts for the energy required for digital data transfer. When considering the campaign's production, possibly involving flights to another continent to shoot the ad, and all other related emissions, the average figure is significantly higher. Advertisers should reflect on this as early as when approving an agency's script. Is this idea truly worth producing? This is one perspective on responsibility, concrete and easy to measure, but I have another.

When we know that up to 90 percent of advertising goes unnoticed, the fact is that many advertisers marketing acts are far away of responsible. Every advertisement's aim, or at least it should be, is to capture a person's attention for a moment. Whether it's two seconds or 90 seconds, it doesn't matter. We are, after all, in a business that fights for people's attention—and consumes their precious time. Some might say we're stealing seconds from people, seconds that all of us have in finite supply. A responsible advertiser evaluates their content from this perspective as well. Does the time we take from people offer anything in return? Any reward for spending time with our brand?

If advertisers considered these two dimensions when creating content—the concrete carbon footprint and genuinely respecting the audience's time—we could talk about *content responsibility*. Let this be the new term for an industry that loves coining them.

CHAPTER 8

The Safe Courageousness

One thing that bothers me in the world of marketing is the word courage, which is proudly displayed in many brand books. It's somewhat awkward that the marketing world somehow redefines courage as something entirely different than what courage means in the real world. And many brands (and especially many people working in marketing) want to create something outstanding. Something that will go down in history. Unfortunately, achieving that is only possible by being courageous on real-world terms. Courage by real-world standards means being willing to fail, to face criticism, to speak about taboos, to shake prevailing thought patterns—and to strike those chords in the human soul that resonate on a deeply human level. I would even say that you're not making courageous acts if you're not a little afraid at the same time. And this is the pitfall into which corporate "courage" often falls. A new standard of courage is created, minimizing risks—and business objectives are met at least roughly, sometimes even quite well. Inside the company, one's own actions are seen as courageous, while the big audience probably won't bat an eye and will forget the brand's message almost immediately. And certainly, nothing iconic is created.

In real life, people are facing truly situations that urge a totally different kind of courage—and the scale is quite broad: the decision to propose and thereby commit to another person for a lifetime, the decision to end a relationship when a shared future is no longer imaginable, combating climate change with personal consumption choices, giving up contraception in the hope of having a child, taking out a large mortgage when the dream home is found, and the decision to end intensive care for a loved one. Real life is full of gigantic emotions and courageous decisions—and that's why the superficial courage prevalent in marketing so rarely leaves any emotional impact on people.

Although I try to write a somewhat different marketing book focusing on practical thinking and examples, it feels necessary to bring another graph onto the stage. Apologies, we will get to the storytelling soon. I once spontaneously sketched out a graph for a client on a flip chart to show how courage, the difficulty of buying ideas, and conversely, the effectiveness of ideas is in some way proportional and related to each other. The basic idea is that the effectiveness of an idea and the difficulty of buying it within the advertiser's organization are directly proportional. And on the other hand, as the uniqueness of the idea increases on a scale of 1 to 10, raising the level becomes exponentially more difficult toward ten. For example, raising the level from an index value 9.5 to 10 is a huge leap—and that's why we see so few of them. And I don't believe that the bottleneck is really on the creative end, even though, of course, teams capable of a level 9 or 10 performance are rare. The real problem is on the buyer's end. It's easy to admire great ideas at Cannes festivals, but it's a very different situation when a completely unique, exceptional, and boundary-breaking idea comes to your desk for the first time in human history—and you have to make the decision whether to proceed with it or not. These ideas inherently feel risky—and require genuine courage. I also started to consider what elements courage includes. Courage always also means risk. If there is no risk of failure, no courage is needed, right? And risk always implies a certain probability. The more courageous, the greater the risk of failure. This is precisely what companies don't want to understand or accept. Often marketers live from campaign to campaign, all of which have tight sales targets and a sort of short-term compulsion to succeed. And that's exactly why we so rarely see anything refreshingly new or courageous. I would like to stake out purely brand building acts or campaigns on every significant marketer's annual calendar, whose aim is to clearly manifest the values the brand is willing to fight for, what the brand's reason for existence is—and to do it in a way that creates a phenomenon, sparks conversations and reactions both for and against. The result is crowds of people who don't have lukewarm feelings toward the brand but are either fans or opponents of the brand. And this is important:

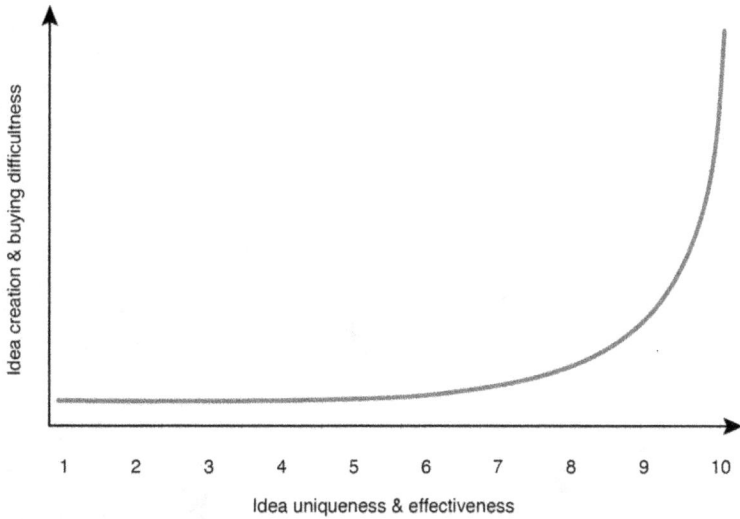

Figure 2 The Idea Curve

Those in charge of the brand must understand that both groups are an incredible asset for them. I'll return to these two groups of people in my creative examples in more detail (Figure 2).

Phew, now the mandatory graphs are done. Let's move forward.

CHAPTER 9

Brands and United Nations Declaration of Human Rights

We are living in times that are critical for humanity in more ways than just environmental issues. Polarization, populism, extremist phenomena, questioning the value of democracy as a societal system to aspire to, and so on. We are, indeed, living through times of historical upheaval. And in many ways, the (Western) world as we've come to know it over the past 70 years is under threat.

At this point, I want to make it clear that I see genuine democracy as undoubtedly the best societal system, if one believes that the values of the United Nations (UN) Declaration of Human Rights are worth defending. And I believe they are. We live in a world where the importance of free democracy and the awareness of human rights are obscured by talks of the aggressive desire of Western countries to spread their own ideology, multipolarity, and so on. And it is precisely at this juncture that Western cultures, who believe in democracy and human rights, should awaken. The UN's Declaration of Human Rights is not an ideology produced by a single culture, but a global effort after World War II to transform the world into a place with less oppression and fewer wars—so that humanity could develop in peace and focus on solving global threats rather than local fears arising from cultural differences. Currently, there are forces whose aim is to blur the UN's Declaration of Human Rights as just one ideology among others. This is extremely dangerous, and the damages it causes are already visible in multiple cultural areas simultaneously. Somewhat surprisingly and simultaneously disheartening has been witnessing the decline of democracy in North America. We have had to witness a situation where North America, the heart of Western power, seems to have abandoned democratic decision making, tramples on human rights, persecutes dissenters—and, overall, tries to turn back the clock to a time when the rich ruled and the poor were valued little more than animals. This is precisely the opposite direction to what the UN's Declaration of Human Rights aims for.

In the marketing field, it sometimes feels that the means to influence societal issues are limited or nonexistent. The thinking goes that you can only try to make the world a better place by running social or public service campaigns. I don't believe that's the case. As said earlier, a person sees between 4,000 and 10,000 commercial messages daily. That's a huge number, although, naturally, most of these messages are aimed at short-term sales. But this flood of messages also has a massive power to change people's values and perspectives. Therefore, some of the Western brands born in democracies have a golden opportunity to channel some of their marketing communications to defend the values based on the Universal Declaration of Human Rights. This would make brands a natural part of societal impact and a counterforce to undemocratic trends. I also believe that for many brands, adopting Western values as part of their brand strategy and marketing communications concept would also be a massive business opportunity. If we consider that large target groups supporting democratic and UN human rights, and compatible values, can be found in North America, South America, Europe, Africa, Asia (excluding China and North Korea), Australia, and New Zealand, we're talking about billions of people. What if some people in these regions don't view democratic development as a positive thing? That's just an asset, as it makes those who do support these values commit even more strongly to the message. A strong counterforce is always an asset from a brand's perspective. This asset just needs to be channeled correctly and not be deterred even by strong resistance.

And rest assured, I'm not writing a book about how every brand should become an activist brand, wagging its finger and sternly trying to fix the world. But if even some brands saw this as an opportunity for positive change—and, selfishly, for defending a market-driven and individual freedom-based societal system that also benefits brands—that would already be an incredible achievement. And now to the main point, the concrete examples, and some rational madness, s'il vous plaît.

PART 2: CASE STUDIES

Nike: Part I—Rethinking the Iconic Marketing Concept

I'll break the pattern right in the beginning: Although most examples in this book are built on an entirely new marketing concept, the following section utilizes an existing concept. And what else could it be than Nike and its Just Do It concept.

When I spoke earlier about courage and how the marketing industry has seemingly created its own standards for what is considered bold, Nike is showing that a brand can also boldly delve into the deep end of humanity. I believe that brands can very well be at the forefront of ultimate truths as measured by real-world standards, provided, of course, that the approach supports the brand's core and brand concept.

As I've already stated Nike is an excellent example of a brand with a clear and strong point of view to this world through the concept Just Do It. In particular, the campaign done with Colin Kaepernick brilliantly demonstrated how Nike's marketing concept could help to take a stance also on a politically charged issue—and create a huge phenomenon that increased the brand's stock value, was a commercial success, and also triggered a strong backlash. What especially warmed my heart was how Nike had prepared for the backlash and used it as a resource to only amplify their message. Negation isn't always an undesirable thing, even though most marketers avoid it like the plague.

Nike's Just Do It marketing concept has, in my opinion, already demonstrated its potential and deserves all the attention, and even admiration; I took on the challenge to find new dimensions for it. And I didn't want to find a new perspective just for the sake of it. I firmly believe it's high time for Nike to shake up its concept a bit. In my opinion, its inspiring top athlete stories have started to go in circles. Yes, work hard and you can achieve anything—make it to the top of the world, become the new Williams sisters, a Super Bowl quarterback, an NBA star, or whatever. But how relatable or genuinely inspiring is that message really for a middle-aged everyday Joe who just wants to get rid of the love handles?

And this is a big strategic shift, not just some short-term gimmick: The Just Do It philosophy could more often take the perspective of the ordinary exerciser, as it did in the early days of launching the concept. Sports marketing has been treading the same path for quite some time, and as a result, sports brands have started to resemble one another in striking ways. Simply put, the success stories of elite athletes are, at their core, quite similar. Blood, sweat, tears, relentless discipline, a committed inner circle, the right genes, and a series of fortunate coincidences. I would argue that the lives of ordinary people are much more diverse—and therefore richer from the storytelling perspective—as long as the lens through which we view them is right and the brand has the courage to tell the most compelling stories. But the big question is: What are the insights we can uncover—those insights that win the hearts of everyday exercisers? And as always, we must dive deep to find the fundamental truths. So, I started thinking about what really gets us to exercise. Why do we exercise in the first place? It can be quite safely assumed that the most significant reason to exercise is to maintain or improve health. Sounds like a given. But sometimes the best part of a given is that it's also the truth. You just must look beyond the obvious, see the obvious in a new light. Why, then, is it important to maintain one's health? You could list endless reasons for this—everyday stamina, weight management, sexual attractiveness, and so on—but I found an insight so big that perhaps for that reason it has gone unnoticed. Or because it's taboo.

Isn't the ultimate reason for exercise that health means the possibility of a fuller life—and on the other hand, a longer life? And it was precisely this question of life and death that I wanted to delve deeper into. I dug up some research to support the idea, and perhaps this insight was the easiest of all the topics in my book to find facts for.

Here is a quote from a study of *British Journal of Sports Medicine* (Gorzelitz et al. 2022):

Weightlifting and aerobic MVPA (moderate to vigorous physical activity) were both independently associated with lower all-cause and CVD (cardiovascular disease) mortality. Observed associations between weightlifting and all-cause mortality did not appear to vary by the participant factors we examined other than sex. Joint models revealed 32% lower all-cause mortality with meeting aerobic MVPA guidelines without any weightlifting; conversely, weightlifting 1–2 times/week was associated with 20% lower all-cause mortality without any aerobic MVPA. In joint models, our data show that weightlifting with most levels of aerobic MVPA was associated with 15–47% lower all-cause mortality.

Quite impactful stuff, I'd say. Who wouldn't want to reduce the risk of premature death by even 47 percent? I believe the reason no commercial entity has seized on this insight is purely due to a lack of courage. On the other hand, whoever could skillfully seize this opportunity could reach a whole new level when it comes to capturing people's attention and engaging them through marketing communications. And I believe that if anyone could rise to this challenge, it would be Nike.

So, I concluded that the strongest statement imaginable, related to exercise, is that *exercise is important because people want to live longer*. Put differently, and a bit more boldly phrased, *exercise is important because people fear death*. At this point, I knew that I was in the presence of something exceptional. Death is, thematically, of course a difficult and in many ways audacious thought, but I was intrigued by the idea that Nike might dare to bring the theme to the table. *Exercise so that you would live longer. Just do it.* Wouldn't that message be quite refreshing and inspiring? Of course, bringing such a big taboo into the focus of the message really requires a lot from the dramatization itself, the way to convey the desired message. And the truth is, everything in marketing communication depends on dramatization. Strategy slides or insights in PowerPoint don't warm the general public one bit.

But it's often also the case that the stronger and more exceptional the conceptual idea itself is, the easier it is also to plan the dramatization. Sometimes it feels like a strong concept practically writes its own stories. That's what happened in this case.

I wrote the first film script on the spot, and I believe it illuminates crystal-clearly why I find this idea so strong. I aimed to create the most emotionally impactful framework possible, so I placed the story within a family context. You'll also notice that I've addressed a very serious topic with an entertaining and even light tone of voice. In my opinion, this is extremely pivotal: A brand can tackle almost any subject as long as the tone is suitable for the brand. It's obvious that although the approach is somewhat light-hearted, it would anger many and provoke some sort of backlash. And, on the other hand, it could generate extremely strong commitment, even change the whole attitude toward exercise, among some people.

The next film story could be published, for example, on Mother's Day, when timeliness would add yet another layer to it. But, of course, the story would also work season independently as a big brand film.

BRAND FILM "Mother"

We are on a street in a cozy neighborhood. However, next to one house, in the shadows, we see a frightening figure—the Grim Reaper himself—leaning against the wall with his scythe beside him. It seems like he's waiting for someone. We cut inside the house, where we see a woman, around 40 years old, dressed in running gear, tying her Nike running shoes in the hallway. She shouts goodbye to her family. A small, about four-year-old girl happily runs into the hallway, and the mother scoops her up for a hug before she closes the front door behind her. The woman puts on her headphones and starts running. From this point on, we hear the audio of cinematic music that increases toward the end.

As the woman turns away from her home street, the Grim Reaper detaches from the shadows and starts running after the woman with a billowing cloak.

Unaware of the death behind her, the woman continues her run, never once looking back. The audience might feel an urge to shout at the woman to run faster as it seems like the Grim Reaper is catching up to her. The scenery changes, and the life-or-death race continues. Until the story reaches its climax: the street ends in a steep staircase. The Grim Reaper seems to pick up speed, as if his prey is trapped. However, the woman starts running up the stairs with determination. In a close-up, we see the woman's feet as her Nike shoes rapidly pound the steps. And there's the unexpected twist: The Grim Reaper's pace starts to slow down, and eventually, he comes to a stop, leaning on his scythe in the middle of the staircase. The Grim Reaper is out of stamina! The woman is in a perfect runner's high state and continues her run at the end of the staircase with a satisfied expression on her face.

A message appears on the screen:

Exercising can reduce the risk of premature death by up to 47 percent.

+ Swoosh + slogan Just Do It

Let's return to the story for a moment. We see the Grim Reaper in front of Nike's flagship store. He tries to enter the shop, but at the door stands a huge security guard shaking his head repulsively. The Grim Reaper turns away with a sigh (Figure 3).

To me, this story is exceptionally strong in many ways. It follows a classic narrative structure while also considering the needs of modern digital channels. In other words, we hook the viewer right from the first seconds by introducing the tension between the Grim Reaper and the mother. Nike is also presented early on, both as a brand and on a product level, when we see the mother in Nike running gear, tying her shoes in the hallway. And what's great is that we don't just claim our products achieve something, but we base a strong statement on scientific fact. And the actual hero is the woman. This makes the manifestation quite compelling. As a small anecdote, I have to mention that I excitedly shared the script I presented above with my wife. I read it out loud, fully immersed in the story. My wife's reaction was somewhat laconic—but from Nike's perspective, absolutely spot on. She simply stated, rather matter-of-factly: "I need new running shoes."

Because my approach is much more than just an ad, a big conceptual idea, the topic can certainly be approached from many other angles than just the film script I've presented. When the conceptual idea is clear, it provides a solid framework for various kinds of storytelling. And since, besides film, brand behavior—actual actions—form the most impactful means of marketing communication, I will next explore the ***Long Live the Athlete idea through a few brand actions.

Active Parent Challenge

Nike could well adopt the perspective that people are increasingly neglecting their health and fitness—and a particularly important target group is

Figure 3 Outrunning the Death

parents living through the "rush years" of raising young families, for whom exercise easily keeps dropping lower on the list of priorities. But isn't the essence of parenthood also the idea that you can be a good, active, and involved parent for as long as possible? This somewhat more serious and profound thought, that children need capable parents, would undoubtedly resonate with the target audience. Nike could establish a program where mothers and fathers who have met certain exercise goals could go on an all-expenses-paid active vacation with the whole family, sponsored by Nike. Perhaps canoeing, horseback riding, hiking, and so on. The current digital platforms of Nike, such as the Nike Training Club and Nike Running Club apps, would serve excellently as the platform for this program. Engaging content and attractive rewards would drive users to the apps, bringing in new business potential. Additionally, this would already serve as a content production platform, as these winning families could be documented on, say, the canoeing trip they won as a prize, and the content could be shared in digital channels. These stories would naturally include the age-old narrative arc of "rags to riches," as a parent fighting back to being physically capable tells precisely this story. And if we take the idea a bit further, this could also serve as a good example of how a brand creates content that is no longer just advertising, but content that competes equally with other paid entertainment. Perhaps a mental reference could be reality series like *The Biggest Loser* or *Ramsay's Kitchen Nightmares*. In this case, it could turn into an engaging reality TV show where parents overwhelmed by the pressures of everyday life—and who have neglected themselves— would undergo training with a well-known fitness coach. In addition to the parents, the show would also focus on their children, grandparents, and other relatives who support the parents on their transformation journey. The result would be a series that people would genuinely want to watch—and one that perfectly aligns with the Just Do It brand concept.

Cheering Is Caring

I wanted to play around with the idea a bit more, so I delved into phenomena related to health and illness. I noticed I was following a train of thought where exercise actually appears as a process of healing for the body. A neglected body is like one gripped by illness, often even literally so, and exercise sort of unleashes the body's own repair mechanism and starts to develop into a healthier direction. However, I didn't want to communicate this too medically but to find some inspiring way to express this idea. I also considered that the support and encouragement from loved ones have a big impact on achieving one's goals—really in all areas of life, but the need for motivation is especially concrete in the realm of exercise. The mere culture around Personal Trainers says a lot about this. But could Nike, for example, find some irresistible way for people to even humorously indicate that they have noticed their loved ones' neglect in the area of exercise—and want to be part of supporting them to reengage with the joy of movement? After pondering this for a while, the idea popped into my head about casts on legs or arms, on which family members or friends have always written encouraging messages for the recovering patient.

And there it was, the idea that would be irresistibly endearing: produce all-white Nike running shoes or training clothes specifically for this purpose for both men and women—and select the surface material in such a way that it's particularly easy to write messages on with markers (of course, all-white running shoes already exist in the collection, which can also be used). We package this as a set that comes with an assortment of colored markers. We launch a campaign perhaps around Mother's or Father's Day and talk about this touching gift idea maybe through influencer marketing. I believe this brand action would have a lot of potential to really make the concept of Long Live the Athlete hit home. It would give people a tool to tell their loved ones that they care about them and want them to stay healthy. And I would think that it would be quite motivating and inspiring to go for a run with, say, cheer messages from one's own children. They are practically running along with you! More visibility for this brand action can be obtained by connecting it to an activation: When you share a picture of your own cheer-message shoes on social media with the hashtag #cheeringiscaring, you could win Nike product prizes or personalized video messages from top athletes sponsored by Nike. Why not even a cheer message from a top athlete written on a T-shirt or running shoes! (Figure 4).

The Fountain of Youth

I wanted to also try out what kind of other brand stories or approaches Long Live the Athlete could generate. If exercise is a sort of fountain of health, then Nike running shoes can directly be compared to this. And when you delve

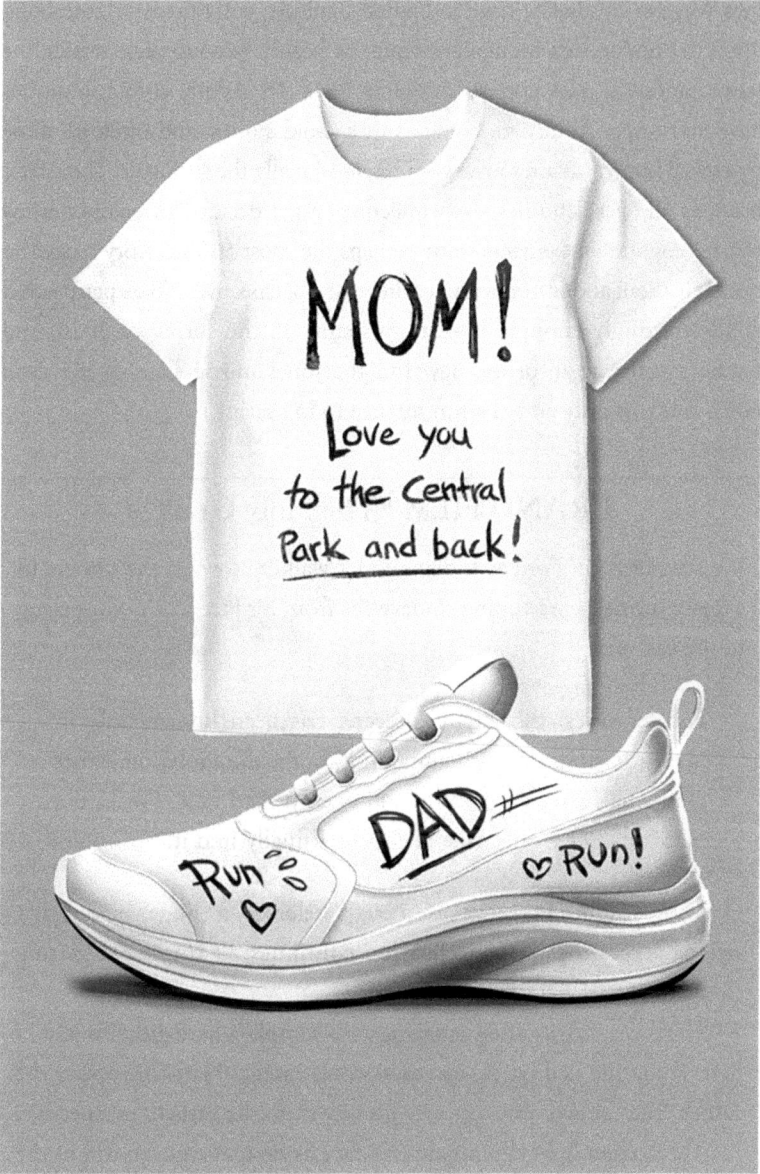

Figure 4 Cheering is Caring

into Western cultural heritage and popular culture, you can't avoid stumbling upon the notion of a fountain of youth or health. Among these stories, the most famous is undoubtedly the Holy Grail. Marketing communications have every opportunity to leverage our age-old stories, and often it's those most well known that resonate with us emotionally the strongest. These have been tested over centuries, even millennia. So, I decided to boldly borrow some recognizable elements from perhaps the most famous story related to the Holy Grail and introduce an entirely new perspective: Nike's perspective.

Interestingly enough, I wrote this story in the spring of 2020, and I wasn't aware at all of the new Indiana Jones movie starring Harrison Ford. But this only added a fun nuance to my script.

BRAND FILM "The Holy Grail"

We see Harrison Ford as Indiana Jones walking toward the camera in a dusty tunnel. He's wiping spiderwebs from his face while whispering to the camera:

> For centuries, this mythical secret has been known only in tales: the story of the Fountain of Youth, the Holy Grail that grants you strength, health, and energy. And now, I'm in the place where we can make history and finally find it.

Harrison suddenly bows as a trap releases a huge blade that sweeps across the tunnel. Harrison continues: "I think I'm getting closer ...."

Harrison arrives at an amazing cave temple where a divine ray of light from the ceiling points to a stone casket. Harrison opens the casket. The camera now captures his face from the casket's perspective.

The golden light illuminates his face as he removes the top of the casket.

HARRISON: This is it. The fountain of youth and health.

Then we finally see inside the casket over the Harrisons shoulder, and the secret is revealed: a pair of brand-new Nike shoes.

The payoff and logo appear on the screen:

Long Live the Athlete.

[or]

Exercising can reduce the risk of premature death by up to 47 percent.
Nike—Just Do It.

After the logo screen, we return to the story for just a couple of seconds. The entire temple mountain is collapsing with huge explosions behind Harrison, who escapes the scene by running at full speed. The camera lowers to show his running feet: He's wearing the new Nikes (Figure 5).

Figure 5 The Holy Grail

The Holy Grail of Public Relations

The idea of the Holy Grail also provides excellent building blocks for actions other than just film. What if Nike were to launch a new running shoe in a teaserlike manner, without initially revealing the brand or the product at all! There would just be a flashy press conference, the content of which is that scientists have found a miracle cure that has been clinically proven to extend lifespan and reduce many diseases. The press conference would comprehensively discuss this wonder method and present numerical values and percentages on how this "cure" affects human physiology. These numerical values would directly correspond to the amazing health benefits of exercise, like the fact of 47 percent lower risk of premature death. Only at the end would it be revealed that behind it all are Nike's new running shoes—which are the secret weapon for finding a healthy lifestyle. Just do it.

Nike, Part II: Moments of Just Do It

When I was working on this idea of Long Live the Athlete, a parallel perspective also emerged on the Just Do It concept. And this often happens when the subject is interesting and, above all, there's time for thoughts to mature and the subconscious is constantly working on the topic. One beautiful day a new idea pops into mind. This is unfortunately rare in creative work: that there's actually time for thoughts to mature and develop. And that's exactly why I've been so happy about this personal project of mine. I've had the good fortune to enjoy the rare luxury of time.

At the core of the Just Do It philosophy is the idea that starting to exercise is difficult because you are your own biggest enemy. We have a natural inclination toward comfort, and when our life is no longer dependent on running after prey, our body and mind try to convince us that it's not worth running for no reason—rather, it's better to save energy. This mechanism is deeply ingrained in our genes, which is why I think Just Do It is such a brilliant concept. It already inherently has a deep psychophysical dimension that challenges our most primal mechanisms of action. I have been amazed and even puzzled that I haven't found a similar analysis of the Just Do It concept. The concept is, indeed, described in the book Shoe Dog, but the interpretation there is quite straightforward— it's about attitude. An attitude rooted in the idea that there's an athlete in you too—if only you straighten up and give yourself a little kick in the butt. Like one of my favorite Nike ads describes it: "Yesterday you said tomorrow. Just do it." However, I haven't found anyone else pondering why exactly that attitude resonates with us so strongly. Perhaps this is precisely one of the reasons why the actions of brands remain so superficial and short-lived in general. Something is found that seems to resonate with recipients, but there's no effort to pause and consider why this is the case. Then, the opportunity to consciously build similar success stories is also lost. But Nike has not been a shooting star because the conceptual thought is so strong—and thank goodness, in marketing, there have been visionaries who understand the value of systematic and long-term commitment.

I dug a bit for scientific evidence to support my idea and stumbled upon paleoanthropologist at Harvard University Daniel Lieberman, who describes the situation just as I had thought in his article: "Our ancestors exerted so much energy hunting and gathering that they sought rest whenever they could. We are predisposed to want to conserve energy."

He continues:

> It is natural and normal to be physically lazy. I predict that hunter-gatherers in the Kalahari or the Amazon are just as likely as 21st century Americans to instinctually avoid unnecessary exertion … the vast majority of people today behave just as their ancestors by exercising only when it is fun (as a form of play) or when necessary.

With this thought in mind, I expanded the perspective a bit and sought relevance from the challenges that modern humans face. I toyed with the idea, therefore, of what else Just Do It could be a precise remedy for. I concluded that natural laziness, love of comfort—and on the other hand, endless options these days in terms of life choices—lead us to suffer from a great curse of indecisiveness. We fail to make decisive decisions and moves in our lives, and thus we unnecessarily close doors behind for ourselves. We close doors behind which there could be a positive change in our lives. In other words, we are our own worst enemy in terms of our development and happiness. This seemed to offer something new and, in a tantalizing way, familiar from the perspective of the Just Do It philosophy. The original psychological strength of the Just Do It concept relies on the truth that we are naturally lazy and therefore have to overcome a significant threshold to go out for a run just to improve our fitness. A new level could be found in the evolution of the Just Do It concept touching people's lives and life choices more broadly.

I also found interesting psychological studies to support my thoughts. Psychologist Ahona Guha encapsulates the issue well:

> Sometimes people forget that not making a choice is in itself a choice, and that the costs of refusing to commit to a course of

action or being unable to sustain action can have heavy costs in the long term. It is very important to live lives directed by choice, not chance, and to make good decisions based on a clear sense of what we value and what we want to explore in life.

She also lists things that make us our own enemies. For example, fear is a very common subconscious reason for not changing one's own life. People are safety oriented, and change is always something unknown. But especially interesting is her thought about self-efficacy:

> Self-efficacy is our belief in our capacity to manage a certain situation or to effect change in our lives. It is probably one of the most vital psychological competencies we can build, because it lies at the heart of our belief that we can change our lives, learn new things, or develop better behaviors and patterns. If we lack this belief, we are likely to experience some learned helplessness and will not even contemplate taking action on making changes we might desire, because we do not fundamentally believe that we will succeed.

Against this backdrop, it is easy and justified to see Nike's brand concept in a new light. The Just Do It concept is a perfect remedy for the psychological reasons previously described for not taking decisive steps in one's life. We could expand the brand philosophy built around sports to encompass all of life. This idea would be dangerous if Just Do It were a new concept. Naturally, at first, it's better to stay more firmly within the sports context and be more relevant to Nike's core business, but once the concept has been ingrained in people's minds through decades of systematic marketing, the idea I've developed would offer entirely new and virgin ground. This way, even a somewhat familiar concept would be invigorated and given an unexpected, yet completely consistent, developmental arc. *At the core of my thought is the realization that, in life, you just need to get over the threshold of inaction and make decisive decisions. Just Do It!*

I've been considering this approach from the perspective of brand relevance, as it would be a mistake to move too far away from the world on which Nike's business is based and with which people are accustomed to associating Nike. I believe I've ultimately found an approach that solves these problems, at least in terms of narrative storytelling in films. In the world of marketing communications, tight creative formats have been proven to be extremely effective. By format here, I mean a narrative formula that always, in some way, repeats the same structure. There are many excellent examples in the world of marketing communications, but one of my all-time favorites is Snickers, whose "You are not you when you are hungry" concept has brilliantly demonstrated the advantages of a tight format. I wanted to create a setup for Nike that starts off blatantly commercial, rooted in Nike's world, so that the surprising shift into a new context is somehow preestablished and doesn't take too great a leap in people's minds. The format I've created also has the advantage of enabling really concise storytelling that would also work well in fast-paced digital channels.

The core of the creative basic idea is this: We are always in Nike's trendy flagship store. We see a person trying on Nike shoes. Once the shoe is on, a shift occurs in the person's mindset, even a somewhat magical "Just Do It" moment. They take their phone in hand and make a call or speak to a friend, family member, or Nike employee who is present during the fitting—and reveals a significant decision in their life or another matter they haven't been able to tackle before. The role of Nike shouldn't be overstated; it's just a subtle trigger that prompts the person to act according to the Just Do It philosophy. However, what the brand is about will not be unclear to anyone, as the context of the events and the presentation of the product itself take care of that. I have chosen a shoe for this, but in principle, the narrative formula could be expanded to other Nike products as well. At least initially, a shoe seems like a natural choice because trying it on doesn't occur in a fitting room and someone else is naturally involved, even a Nike employee.

Moments of Just Do It

Next, I present a series of short stories that follow a strict narrative format—and through systematic repetition would become ingrained in people's minds as super-recognizable advertising concepts.

SCRIPTS

Paris

We are in Nike's flagship store. An older lady tries on Nike shoes. Once the shoe is on, she says to the Nike employee who has helped her: "I've always wanted to see the Eiffel Tower. It's never too late; I'm going to book the trip today." The message on the screen: Nike—Just Do It.

Proposal

A young woman is trying on Nike shoes with her mother. Once the shoe is on, she says to her mom: "I've been thinking about my relationship with Fred. He's the man of my life, and I'm going to propose to him this weekend." The message on the screen: Nike— Just Do It.

Son

A man tries on a Nike shoe in Nike's flagship store. Once the shoe is on, he takes out his phone and calls: "Dad, I've never told you this before: even if you don't realize it yourself, you're a good man and have always been a role model for me. I love you." The message on the screen: Nike—Just Do It.

(This concept also offers many opportunities for seasonal storytelling; for instance, the previous story could be published well on Father's Day.)

Cupido

A young girl is trying on shoes with her dad. A friendly female salesperson has helped with the fitting. Once the shoe is on, she says to the salesperson: "Hey, you seem really nice, and my dad has been pretty lonely after mum decided to become an angel. Would you go out for coffee with dad sometime?" The dad and the shop assistant look at each other, and a faint smile appears in their eyes. The message on the screen: Nike—Just Do It.

New Path

A young man tries on a shoe. Once the shoe is on, he takes out his phone and calls: "Mom, I've realized I'm in the wrong field. I'm going back to school." The message on the screen: Nike—Just Do It.

Big Step

A couple in their 30s is trying on shoes. The woman gets the shoe on and says to her partner: "Listen, I feel like I'm ready. Let's try to have a baby." The message on the screen: Nike—Just Do It.

While the creative concept works well for dramatizing ordinary people's turning points in life, the format can also add layers and seek differentiation in many different ways. Here are a few examples.

One More Year

LeBron James tries on a shoe at the Nike store. Once the shoe is on, he says to the young employee who has helped him find the right shoe: "You know what, I'm gonna play at least one more year." The message on the screen: Nike—Just Do It.

This would also be an opportunity for a massive PR stunt, as some star athlete from Nike's roster could announce the continuation or end of their career through this creative concept. The career ending would be even more unconventional Just Do It story. The next example is from the "something else" department.

Tellus We Want

A slimy, multilimbed alien tries on a shoe at a Nike store. When the shoe slips onto an oddly shaped, elastic limb, the alien touches its temple and contacts somewhere in space. He speaks in a strange language, which is subtitled: "This is the planet we want, start the operation Tellus." The message on the screen: Nike—Just Do It (Figure 6).

Figure 6 Just Do It Moments

Brand Behavior/Products as a Message

Nike shoes, or why not other products, could be used as a message also in this second approach: A person who has long been hesitating over some significant matter and has not been able to make a decisive decision could receive Nike shoes from their family or friends. Nike could create a campaign-style shoebox with space on the lid to write a message, for example, "Hey, it's really time for you to apply to med school now. Just Do It." "She's a keeper, propose to her!" The motivational text could be written directly in Nike's online store and would automatically be printed on the shoebox. In this way, Nike's "Just Do It" attitude would have an entirely different opportunity to become a part of people's lives. The shoes would no longer literally be just shoes, or sportswear just clothes; they would be something more. They would be message batons adapted to people's lives with Nike's brand message.

Steps of Life

I believe that the previous examples effectively showcase the inspiring and encouraging side of the approach. They demonstrate how one can easily derive a multiyear and highly recognizable continuum from philosophy. But as I realized during the conceptual phase, the Just Do it philosophy can be examined through multiple psychological insights. And in these next thoughts, I'm making a conscious choice: they are no longer strictly tied to the context of sports, which is naturally quite a mental leap for a sports brand. The idea here is that the Just Do It concept is already so well established that everyone essentially knows the context in which Nike operates. These ideas draw from deeper sources *yet remain entirely true* to Nike's brand concept. There's certainly a reason why brands, in general, don't step outside their own category, but since this book is more of a thought experiment, I can take creative liberties. However, I don't take those liberties lightly. My goal is simply to find the most impactful brand stories that still adhere to the brand concept—just in a rather unexpected way. And fundamentally, that's only possible because the brand concept itself is so strong.

Studies of lifespan psychology have shown that one of the biggest regrets people have on their deathbeds are the actions not taken and decisions not made. People even regret the things they didn't do more than the decisions or actions that later turned out to be mistakes! This thought provides an interesting starting point and another approach to the concept Just Do it. For example, the article "The Temporal Pattern to the Experience of Regret" (Gilovich and Medvec 1994) summarizes the idea well: "Feelings of regret in the long-term are more likely for decisions involving inaction; that is, choosing not to do something."

Another extremely interesting study shows that the most long-lasting regrets are related to those unmade decisions and actions that prevented us from becoming the people we ideally envisioned ourselves to be (Davidai and Gilovich 2018).

I also found wise words in an article by former health care professional turned writer Grace Bluerock, who describes the regrets she's heard from people on their deathbeds: "Many felt that a fear of failure caused them to play it too safe. They knew that they could have had richer, more fulfilling lives had they taken some risks and disturbed the status quo."

This thought intrigued and followed me for weeks. I thought that from a storytelling perspective, there's something uniquely compelling here. I considered the randomness of life and how often a seemingly minor event—at least now it happens—can have life-altering consequences. I also played with the idea that if we had the courage to seize all the opportunities life offers, what a life that would be. On the other hand, and here I believe lies an emotionally impactful perspective in its sadness, the missed opportunities, the steps not taken, offer a chance for truly touching storytelling. This approach is intentionally very different from the previous one. If the former creative approach was purely entertaining and demonstrated through humor and even audacity where the Just Do it attitude can lead us as individuals, the purpose now is to touch people deeply and make them reflect on their own lives and choices. I also wanted to create a completely different atmosphere, one rarely used in marketing communications: even a poignant mood. With the right execution, this type of dramatization can be incredibly effective and impactful. It does not aim solely for a good and uplifting mood, but it gives the brand an even larger role at the end of the story. And it would be something totally new in the context of sports marketing—that's for sure.

BRAND FILM "Steps of Life"

We show grainy footage from around the 1950s (not necessarily an archive film, we can actually record the scene and edit the footage in post-production to make it look old). Throughout the film, we only see a toddler who has just learned to walk. First, a close-up of the child's feet taking tentative steps, then from the front, a shot of the child walking hesitantly with arms outstretched, following the camera.

We hear an older man telling the story as a voice-over:

Those first steps I took were actually the easiest ones. After those, there were years when I didn't take any steps. I didn't take that one step to ask that girl to the prom; I didn't take the step my teacher advised me to take after college; I didn't take the step to make peace with my dad in his last months. I didn't take the step to quit the job I hated. I didn't take the step to open the door of a dancing class even though my body was built for that, and dancing was my secret but true passion. All those steps I didn't take were simply because I was afraid of something—something that really didn't exist, fear that was just in my head. I can see that so clearly now.

The slogan and logo appear on the screen: *Just Do it* + *Swoosh* (Figure 7).

I've been contemplating this story a lot. It's an atypical advertising story in the sense that it's bleak and poignant. It's a story of a lost unique opportunity, whereas brands usually prefer to operate solidly within the inspiring and uplifting realm. But perhaps that's what makes it unique. Something we haven't seen in quite a while. I'm fairly certain this kind of a story wouldn't necessarily receive very good ratings in pretesting, as the mood at the end of the story is melancholic. However, a bold brand storyteller might see potential in this precisely because of that. At the very least, it awakens and hopefully makes one think of life as a fleeting moment to be utilized in every possible way. And to put all one's potential on the line. Deep down, it is precisely an inspiring point of view! But as stated, it first takes its audience out of their comfort zone, shakes them up a bit—yet ultimately provides a tool, its own brand, as the key to navigating this uncomfortable situation.

However, the previous creative concepts demonstrate the many ways Just Do It could be reinvented. It could still embody a strong, inspiring attitude, but in a completely new way—and also set a new direction in the rather clichéd field of sports marketing.

Figure 7 Steps Never Taken

Virgin Atlantic: The Brand That Prevents World War III

The highest attainable goal a brand can set for itself is that people commit to the brand because it strongly represents certain values. When choosing the brand, the individual is also showing that they represent these values. Thus, choosing between brands becomes a choice between values. I want to emphasize at this point that a value choice doesn't necessarily mean only profound or serious values, conventionally understood "purpose". Overcoming oneself can be a value, or even taking a humorous approach to the world. *I chose this brand because I want to show that I have a sense of humor.* That's also a choice of value.

But relating to my earlier thought that there are forces in this era that threaten humanity's positive development toward a more tolerant, equal, and free world, I decided to build an example of a marketing communications concept that would take a strong stance on this phenomenon. However, I also wanted to find facts to back my thinking. Though everyone has been able to sense worrying signs with their own eyes, this following graph, for example, is quite arresting. According to this graph, the index value of political polarization has more than doubled in North America in a surprisingly short period. Practically, the growth of polarization throughout the twentieth century has been negligible, and the trend has even been decreasing in several countries. What caught my attention in particular is that the world's index value barely rose during World War II but is currently much higher than during the war years, and the curve is sharply rising (Figure 8).

We have seen that polarization, segregation, and a certain black-and-white thinking have reared their heads everywhere in the Western world. For example, North America is so divided that many experts even consider a civil war as a possible development. If this is not frightening, I really don't know what is. That's why I've been pondering what brands could do about it.

POLARIZARION IN THE WORLD AND THE UNITED STATES SINCE 1900

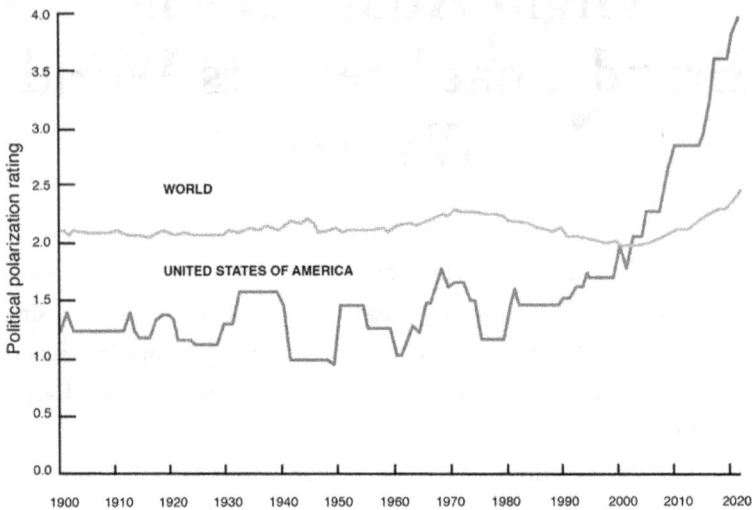

Source: Coppedge, Gerring, Lindberg, and Teorell et al., "V-Dem Dataset Version 11.1"

Figure 8 Polarization Chart

I remember sitting in the auditorium at the Cannes Lions Festival in the summer of 2022, listening to Ukraine's president deliver a speech to us marketing professionals via video link. While the pain was palpable due to Russia's full-scale invasion just a few months earlier, the speech still left me feeling somewhat empty. Zelensky had the idea that advertisers could somehow help Ukraine's cause, but as I thought about it, I realized that he didn't have fully developed tools for how the world could support a nation under attack. His message was a painful plea for help, but one that was somewhat difficult to grasp. Of course, brands can try to raise money or show support for Ukraine in other ways, but very few have actually done so. And I understand why—taking a direct political stance is suitable for only a handful of brands.

But the undeniable fact that global polarization has been accelerating at an alarming rate gave me a new perspective on the entire issue. Now that full-scale war is also in Europe, and the Western alliance is under strain, more and more people are becoming utterly exhausted by forces that fuel hatred and division. I believe that a counterforce is already emerging.

And here is what Zelensky's speech lacked: a clear vision on how this cultural shift should be framed in a way that also makes sense businesswise? The people who are tired of hatred and polarization—tens, if not hundreds, of millions in Western countries—represent enormous business potential. If a brand were to provide real tools for expressing this frustration, it would also be a commercial opportunity. And I can't help but recall Bill Bernbach's wisdom: A brand must stand for something. When you stand for something, you will find both supporters and detractors—and both groups are valuable. The times we are living in right now offer brands an unprecedented opportunity for engagement.

By the spring of 2022, I had already been developing a creative concept for Virgin Atlantic for over a year, and piece by piece, everything started to fall into place. So, let's get to it.

I have always admired Richard Branson for his visionary thinking and straightforwardness. He is genuinely a doer, someone who can bring brand strategy into practice. Because nothing is more miserable than beautiful platitudes in the boardrooms; ideas that are never verified in practice. Virgin Group's vision is "Changing Business for Good." And Virgin Group also verifies this in practice through numerous wonderful projects. I was left wondering that, in this regard, Virgin Group's airline Virgin Atlantic has remained somewhat superficial, at least in terms of marketing communication. And then I began to consider air travel as a business overall and started digging into some background. I've noticed that creativity is often completely misunderstood. The stereotype is that it's some divine moment of inspiration that emerges from a vacuum. In reality, creating something abstract is very much a process of research, immersion, and analysis of all the material you uncover—and thinking, above all. That's exactly what happened in this case. I stumbled upon something in the depths of the Internet completely by chance, and it hit me like a slap in the face: Wake up, here's an insight so strong you may never come across similar again!

It was an article that illuminated the background as to why aviation kerosene is tax-free. The story behind this decision is fascinatingly immense. After World War II, the Chicago Convention decided to exempt aviation kerosene from taxes, stating that *Tax exemption on kerosene and the support to international civil aviation could contribute to trust, friendship and understanding between the nations and peoples of this world.*

I read this sentence twice, and then a few more times after that. I knew I wouldn't encounter a stronger insight anytime soon. So, a decision was made after World War II to promote travel because it would foster mutual understanding between people. In other words, long-distance travel was made cheaper for ordinary people to possibly prevent a third world war! I was awestruck. This 80-year-old insight feels frighteningly relevant today. I decided that a marketing communication concept must be built around this—and that Virgin Atlantic would be the perfect match, as the underlying group's purpose of Changing Business for Good supports this insight perfectly.

This, in my opinion, is a brilliant example of the importance of strong insight: Once you find it, it feels like you're sliding down a slide and everything flows almost effortlessly afterward. Virgin Atlantic could fully embrace the entire philosophy of the Chicago Convention, as it is entirely relevant to their industry, business, vision—and the spirit of the times. The idea of travel's positive impact on preventing polarization, eliminating prejudices, and fostering mutual understanding between people would be an immediately usable and incredibly powerful brand statement. And once this statement gets ingrained in people's minds, buying an airplane ticket will never be the same again. By choosing Virgin Atlantic, people would show that they have made a strong value choice, representing certain values, advocating for unity, and striving to prevent conflicts.

But first, the essential question: Is the Chicago Convention's resolution psychologically justified? Is it true? Mark Twain's immortal quote from his book *Innocents Abroad* came to mind: "Travel is fatal to prejudice, bigotry, and narrow-mindedness." Now I just had to find the scientific basis for this. And I did. I found an excellent study called "Does Travel Broaden the Mind? Breadth of Foreign Experiences Increases Generalized Trust." One of the authors, Jiyin Cao, explains the key takeaway (as quoted in a PsyPost article):

> We compared two aspects of foreign experiences: the number of countries one visits (breadth) and the length of time one spends abroad (depth) and explored which one plays a critical role in the process. Across five studies, using different research methods including a longitudinal study, we found that breadth but not depth of foreign experiences increases generalized trust," Cao added. "In other words, the more countries one travels, the more trusting one is. Breadth is important here, because breadth provides a great

level of diversity in people's foreign travel experiences, allowing them to reach such a generalized assumption.

Another experiment of theirs added an interesting new dimension to the relationship between increased trust and travel: Visiting places that are unfamiliar and different appears to be a key factor. In their final experiment, Cao and her colleagues found those who visited places less similar than their homeland became more trusting than those who visited places more similar to their homeland.

After reading these studies, I could quite confidently state that the insight is also scientifically supported, but what kind of concerns would this kind of statement raise? What risks would be involved? If the brand takes such a strong stance on the current polarized world, doesn't it risk alienating a segment of potential air travelers? Let's examine this through the lens of the North American market. If we simplify a bit, this marketing communication concept based on the philosophy of the Chicago Convention would align more with Democratic values but would certainly also resonate with more moderate Republicans. In North America, there were 252 million adults over 18 years of age in 2020 and about 80 million registered Democrats. It's fairly safe to assume that this message could strongly appeal to 100+ million adults—a rather nice business potential, I would say. And if even some of these millions of people start thinking that choosing an airline could be a value-based decision that is also an external statement, we can see the value that a strong brand concept can have. When a brand takes a clear stance, it, of course, causes resistance among some people but also fosters strong engagement among others. Additionally, given that young adults have a more liberal and open view of the world, there would easily be an opportunity here to reach and engage critical young target groups for the future.

In the end, Virgin Atlantic's goal would be no more and no less than what the Chicago Convention aimed for: to prevent the next international conflict. Now, in the spring of 2025, the situation has horrifically deteriorated as Europe is engulfed in a bloody war that violates numerous international laws. On the other hand, themes of unity and tolerance, peacebuilding, and breaking down prejudices will become more critically necessary in the coming years than they have been for decades. And the more I think about it, the more certain I am that there are an increasing number of people in the world who are utterly fed up with politics that seeks to divide and polarize. I believe—and hope—that this could become the next megatrend, at least among the educated and historically aware, regardless of whether a person comes from a conservative or liberal value base.

How relevant is this conceptual idea actually for Virgin Atlantic—and most importantly, how does this idea translate into communication that aligns with the Virgin Atlantic brand? I believe I have now justified that this approach has business potential, but now it's time to talk about the brand. I am fully aware of Virgin Atlantic's brand personality and tone of voice. It doesn't seem appropriate for Virgin Atlantic to adopt a gloomy approach or wag a finger in a preachy manner. However, even a deep and serious theme can be presented in an entertaining and uplifting way. Virgin Atlantic looks to the future optimistically, viewing it brightly both from humanity's perspective and its own business outlook. Virgin Atlantic (like Virgin Group behind it) aims primarily to inspire and lead the world toward a better future through positivity. As stated, Virgin Group's purpose of "Changing Business for Good" serves as a perfect foundation for a strong brand statement. But I have noticed that missions of this kind can easily produce very bland or even clichéd marketing communication. A world-embracing thought can easily appear as mere platitudes, but engaging and outstanding dramatization always demands a counterforce, a contrast. The real challenge lies in turning a lofty idea into compelling communication. And it's this challenge I wanted to take on.

I crystallized this marketing communication concept, which springs from the philosophy of the Chicago Convention, into a formulation suitable for Virgin Atlantic. Sometimes it's best to say things quite directly, especially if the idea is already clear from the outset. Unnecessary gimmicks may only weaken or obscure the message. And because traveling is medicine against segregation and polarization, it can be seen as a unifying element—mentally and physically. Therefore, the conceptual thinking could be summarized into the following idea:

Virgin Atlantic—*The Unifying Company*

I truly believe that Virgin Atlantic could provide people with this brand concept a tool to demonstrate that they stand against this destructive zeitgeist. That they are advocating for open-minded and humane values. Virgin Atlantic could have a crystal-clear position in this world: It stands for unity.

But as is always the case with marketing, only actions matter. How do we tell the most compelling, distinct, and brand-relevant story based on our conceptual idea?

I'll start with film narratives, as research shows that films build the strongest emotional connection between brands and their audiences (people rarely discuss Internet banners with the same passion as they do about Super Bowl commercials). I've created a few very different approaches just to show that there are always multiple angles to consider. I've used Virgin Group founder Richard Branson in several dramatizations, as he is undoubtedly an invaluable brand asset for Virgin Group. When you see Richard, you immediately know which brand (or at least brand family) you're dealing with. This is particularly important in digital channels, where the story needs to quickly align with the brand. However, I don't believe in rubbing the brand too overtly in the viewer's face—a more subtle and suggestive approach can work perfectly well if the story is good. I've strived in all the narratives to create a visually compelling world right from the first frame so that the story pulls the viewer in and makes the advertising unskippable.

The first story is brazenly straightforward. Virgin Atlantic's staff and fleet are likened to a force that has the potential to change the world. There's a certain paradox in the setup, as this kind of behavior is usually seen in historical war films portraying armies or troops. However, in this case, the army is on the side of peace and unity.

BRAND FILM "Giving Wings to the Dreams"

We are seeing hundreds of Virgin Atlantic personnel standing in their red uniforms in a straight-line. Dozens of Virgin aircrafts stand behind the line of personnel creating a visually epic scene. Richard Branson walks in front of them like Maximus in the movie *Gladiator*, having his "battle speech."

RICHARD: We are living in the strange times where the hatred is rising, and they are building walls again. What do we do to the walls?

The personnel replies as a massive chorus: WE WILL FLY OVER THEM!

RICHARD: There are people dreaming of a less separated world. What do we have to give their dreams?

PERSONNEL: WE WILL GIVE THEM WINGS!

RICHARD: In the times like these, what are we standing for?

PERSONNEL: WE STAND FOR UNIFYING!

A text appears on the screen:

In the separated world, travelling has the power to unify.

[or]

Travelling is a medicine against the polarized world.

Logo + brand promise appears on the screen: Virgin Atlantic—The Unifying Company (Figure 9).

Figure 9 The Speech

The following story is a small tribute to Johnny Walker's iconic manifesto film. I also wanted to elevate a historical background from the Chicago Convention to the core of the story, because it is the essence of the whole marketing concept.

The original script was written before Russia's full-scale attack on Ukraine, but in my opinion, this story is even more powerful now. However, it's very important that the opening scene is clearly a time travel to the time of World War II, not a scene from the present.

BRAND FILM "Unifying Walk"

Richard Branson—dressed in a World War II soldier costume—is walking through a war field and speaking directly to the camera. In the background, bombs are falling, tanks are firing, and men are running from trenches. The quality of this scene should be on par with the movie *1917*. Despite the chaos in the background, Richard remains calm and tells an engaging story:

> World War II was a human catastrophe born from a polarized world and divided nations. Afterwards, we vowed never to let it happen again. In 1944, the Chicago Convention was established to promote air travel to foster cultural exchange, friendship, and understanding among nations.

Cut to the twenty-first century, Richard is now walking with his casual outfit through a crowd chanting, "Build that wall! Build that wall!"

Moving against the tide of people, Richard continues: "Yet recently, something has changed, and the world is more polarized than it has been in decades. We find ourselves on the brink of war once more. This cannot continue."

Now we see Richard strolling through a wide, empty field as he continues: "The world is going mad, but I believe that the travelling has the healing power, just like Chicago Convention believed. And the more the world is separated, the more we stand for unifying. Because travelling is all about unifying."

The camera zooms out, revealing that Richard is walking at the end of a runway. A Virgin A380 takes off behind him, soaring over him and the camera. Cut to a shot of the Virgin A380 gliding gracefully through a clear sky.

Logo + brand promise appears on the screen: Virgin Atlantic—The Unifying Company

For a long time, I thought these two stories delivered the message pretty nicely. But as time went on, I felt a compelling need to find new perspectives. To somehow raise the bar, make something simpler, yet grander. Bolder and more iconic. Something that wouldn't just be an ad.

I found myself mulling over an idea that's intrigued me since my teenage years. It's a simple realization that the world's absolute evilest people—dictators, serial killers, and so on—were also once children. What kind of children were they? Were they completely innocent? What dreams and wishes did they have? I saw in this an opportunity to tell a story that is rooted in the present yet timeless. This thought led to a dramatization that I believe is something unprecedented and intriguing in a human way. And, most importantly, it is painfully relevant.

I wanted to tell the story of a dictator but through a time-travel lens, where we hear him speaking about his hopes and dreams when he was just a child. With today's technology, we can create an amazing deepfake character who is completely recognizable, but in this case, is a 10-year-old version of a well-known dictator of our time. I won't mention names, as it's not necessary in the film either; people will recognize a skillfully crafted character.

BRAND FILM "Iron Curtain"

We see a bit of grainy footage, where a 10-year-old boy who astonishingly resembles a well-known, aggressive dictator of our time speaks directly to the camera in Russian. He's radiantly enthusiastic, sincere, and innocent in his speech:

Even though some people may be evil, the world isn't evil. I believe the world is good. And I want to get to know the whole

> world, its wonders, all the interesting people, nations, and their ways of life. What could be better than getting to know this wonderful planet we live on?
>
> The camera pulls back and zooms out of a vintage tube TV where the boy continues speaking. Richard Branson has been watching the TV and now turns toward the camera. There's pain in Richard's voice:
>
> What could we have avoided if this boy had been able to keep his innocence and see the world? What if he hadn't grown up behind the Iron Curtain? Let's make sure future generations get to experience what this boy could only dream of.
>
> The logo and brand promise appear on the screen: Virgin Atlantic— The Unifying Company

And once I had embarked on this path, I simply had to entertain the idea of another figure, not quite a dictator (yet), but certainly a highly controversial character. Who, moreover, seems to be popping back into the world's spotlight like the famous roly-poly doll. Even though in this story too, we could end up seeing Richard Branson delivering the final sentence, I decided to opt for a simpler conclusion in this script. I believe it's important that the same story can be told from the same starting points, even without Branson. This story naturally developed a perspective that seamlessly supports the unifying theme.

BRAND FILM "The Path"

We see a piece of somewhat grainy footage from the early 1950s. An eight-year-old boy, whose features strikingly resemble Donald Trump, speaks directly to the camera as if in an interview situation. He speaks sincerely and completely innocently:

> My family comes from the old continent, Scotland, and Germany. It's incredibly exciting how both of my parents'

families decided to move here across the great sea and find a new life. How astronomically small was the probability that my parents would find each other! And what's even more amazing, they found each other, even though they represented enemy nations during the war years! When I grow up, I too want to travel with an open mind and let fate decide where my path leads.

Text appears over the image: "Let travelling keep your mind open."

The logo and brand promise appear on the screen: Virgin Atlantic—The Unifying Company

This is intentional: I have dramatized the concept *The Unifying Company* in many different ways. Some of it might be more traditional advertising stuff, but the aim here is also to demonstrate that a creative concept can always be dramatized in countless ways. Sometimes it feels like creative teams quickly latch onto one creative direction and shut their minds off to other possibilities. Remember to play, tease your mind, and decide to find a couple of new perspectives even if you feel that you already have some masterpieces on the table.

Brand Behavior

The theme of unification offers myriad ways to make compelling brand actions for Virgin Atlantic. These aren't mere commercials; they help people deeply understand what the airline truly stands for.

Social Experiment

I find the theme of unification extremely interesting, especially through brand actions. If Virgin Atlantic could bring together two people with completely different worldviews and prove that they can find common ground, that would be more powerful than any scripted ad. It felt intuitive that this is a unique opportunity for a brand action. Traveling is very much about meeting new people and new cultures. But on a smaller scale, even an airplane is a place where you can encounter a new random person and spend several hours just a few inches away from them. It's a totally unique laboratory and a great framework for a human experiment. So, the idea would be to seat people with opposite worldviews next to each other on a long flight—and their conversation would be documented with multiple cameras. This kind of social experiment, of course, requires that we're prepared to do several tests because there's no guarantee that the outcome will always be fruitful in any way. But at best, the result is an interesting documentary that can be shared in many different channels in various formats. It would be great to show that, despite wildly different starting points, people are surprisingly similar underneath.

I also wanted to create lighter brand actions that would still be true to the main idea of the unifying power of travel. The following ideas will bring people together in very concrete ways and aim for maximum emotional reactions.

Unified Family

Christmas is an interesting season for brands in many ways. On one hand, it's a huge commercial opportunity—on the other, people attach big emotions to it. Picture this: A mom is away on a business trip abroad during Christmas. She sits in her hotel room on Christmas Eve, missing her family like crazy. Then, knock, knock on her door. She thinks it's room service—BUT surprise, it's her hubby and kiddos standing there with bags of Christmas gifts! You could add some extra holiday sparkle to this branding stunt by also bringing in Christmas food, a Christmas tree, and so on. To be honest, the previous idea feels somewhat like a seen cliché, and I pondered for a long time whether it deserves a place in this book. It has something slightly nauseatingly sentimental about it. On the other hand, perhaps one has become a bit of a cynical adman who fears sentimentality too much. But let's spread some more sugar-coating, now that we've started: You could pull off the same kind of heartwarming trick outside of Christmas too. Say, for an exchange student who's on the other side of the world, pining away. There are as many potential stories as there are people separated from their loved ones because of work, studies, or other reasons. And Virgin Atlantic can be the one to bring all these people together. It's like an endless well of emotional stories, perfect for filling up social media channels.

Cargo That Unifies

So, what about air cargo, which is a big deal for airlines. We could totally spin a story about roses picked in the Netherlands, flown in the belly of a Virgin Atlantic plane to Japan, where they end up in a beautiful wedding bouquet. It's a bit of a fresh take but totally relevant to The Unifying Company theme.

Thinking Big

In marketing, a well-known and excellent guideline is to "Think Big." So, don't get stuck in small thinking; stretch your thoughts as big as possible. Even if the final implementation doesn't reach the original idea's flight altitude, the result is likely to be at a higher level than an idea born from traditional starting points. So, I wanted to apply a Think Big approach. What would be the greatest achievement that Virgin Atlantic and Richard Branson could accomplish? For example, could Richard Branson invite the prime ministers of Russia and Ukraine (if not the presidents) for a negotiation that would take place on a Virgin Atlantic plane? (Once the war has reached the point where Ukraine wants to negotiate.) Or could Richard invite the chairpersons of Republicans and Democrats in the United States to a meeting aiming to find ways to curb a divided nation and polarization? As long as the leading thought stems from the theme of unification, the sky's the limit. Pun intended.

And at a slightly lower flight altitude, but still as a very interesting PR move, Richard Branson could invite some people who are known for looking at the world from different perspectives onto his plane to create an interesting discussion. At best, we could see people who are very different in their starting points find surprising unifying themes, perhaps even shedding prejudices, but above all, interesting encounters. Imagine, for example, Elon Musk and Jeff Bezos discussing in a conversation panel facilitated by Richard Branson 10 km up in the sky?

The Emotional Engagement as an Outcome

At its best, the unifying concept would lead to a setup, where people would use Virgin Atlantic's brand as a spokesperson to convey their own values. I dream of a situation where people would share pictures of their Virgin Atlantic plane ticket on social media as a statement and a small gesture of flipping off polarization and prejudices. Wouldn't it be great if choosing an airline could convey that you're not a narrow-minded reactionary jerk?

On the other hand, a bold brand could also give a voice to the opposition and perhaps create a series of interviews on social media, where the interviewees would underline unconsciously the importance and necessity of Virgin Atlantic's Unifying mission with their own narrow-minded attitude toward this world.

In any case, I am fully convinced that when Virgin Atlantic starts to be seen as a strong advocate for certain values—and people start using the brand to highlight their own convictions—it would inevitably also be a commercial success story.

Tesla: Part I—How a Brand That Doesn't Advertise Advertises

To be honest, at one point, I almost deleted this entire chapter. Then I had second thoughts. While the world has changed, and some of this chapter's content now feels absurd in the spring of 2025—almost like a relic from a far more innocent time—I still see a lot of value in it. If you look beyond Tesla as a brand, you can recognize mechanisms here that are genuinely unique and even revolutionary. But sadly, I have no choice but to rewrite the beginning of this chapter. Now, in the spring of 2025, the world has turned upside down, and Elon appears to me as a completely different figure than he did at the beginning of this writing process. I believe I wrote this Tesla section back in 2021, and I think I share the same experience with many others: at that time, Tesla still seemed like a progressive and intriguing project, led by a somewhat eccentric "mad scientist." I have watched with sadness as he has slipped into a position where he reinforces polarization and supports forces that seek chaos, hate and even oppose democracy.

I want to make it clear that I believe more strongly than ever that the UN Declaration of Human Rights is a fundamental value that Western nations must cherish and defend—by all means necessary, if required. However, since Tesla's significance in the electrification of transportation is undeniable, I will not try to replace it with another brand in this section.

Let this also serve as a reminder of how rapidly our world is changing. Let's keep a cool head and believe in the good—without falling into naive idealism. Since the concepts and creative ideas I present are speculative, you can imagine a different brand in place of Tesla. I leave that to the reader's imagination. And then, let's move forward to the content.

The most impactful ways to create an emotional bond between a brand and people are either through a film or a brand action. Often, these overlap a bit, as the actual impact of a brand action may affect a relatively limited number of people, but the action is documented in an interesting way, perhaps in the video format and this story is published and broadcasted to the public through various media channels.

Tesla felt like a fertile brand when I wanted to dive into the deep end of brand actions, as Elon Musk has made an apparently unshakable decision not to do traditional advertising for Tesla. It has been a success story precisely because the product itself follows the basic formula of good marketing: It brings a completely unique perspective to this world and therefore piques people's interest. A four-wheel smooth interface has gained massive attention and changed the market. Tesla cars themselves are a marketing action. Therefore, I've encountered amusing situations at work when someone has questioned the marketing department's demands for increasing the media budget, pointing out that Tesla doesn't do advertising. Why should we? But if you think of marketing traditionally through the four P's, the product is one of these. How much has Tesla invested in this one P? A quick Google search shows that Tesla's research & development budget has been around three to four billion dollars in recent years. How many invest anything close to such sums in any of the marketing P's? I digress a bit from the topic, but this is too tantalizing to ignore: when I'm asked why we must do brand storytelling, or marketing communications, when Tesla doesn't do it, one could rightfully ask, doesn't Tesla actually do brand storytelling? I think that Tesla's story is Elon Musk's story, which is perhaps the most classical combination of ancient Greek storytelling archetypes: 1. Quest (Musk's mission is to save humanity first by electrifying transportation and then by establishing colonies on Mars). 2. Rags to Riches (although Musk's origins are far from poor, he is, nevertheless, a classic example of an individual's rise from a fairly ordinary life to international spotlight). So quite imaginative stories are at the core of Tesla's brand, albeit strongly personified in its founder, but stories nonetheless. This creative madman's and genius's magic dust falls on all Tesla buyers. They are not just buying a car; they are building humanity's future on Mars. Few brands tell such stories, got to say.

But back to Earth. The electric car market is now catching up to Tesla, and new ways to maintain people's interest are needed. So, I was left pondering how Tesla could get the spotlight back on itself with some method of brand behavior? What kind of action could once again shake up the market and create a jaw-dropping reaction: can that even be done?

The original idea behind Tesla was to reinvent the entire passenger transport business. I wanted to stay on this radical train of thought and continue Tesla's unique line. But first, we need to delve into the currents of time and into the world into which Tesla was born. What human motives lie behind Tesla's success? And what kind of psychological insights could Tesla utilize in the future?

The fundamental attractors of Tesla are its progressiveness. Tesla shakes up an industry that has remained largely unchanged since the time Ford's Model T was invented. I believe that this shaking of the status quo has a much bigger psychological impact than the inherent eco-friendliness of electric cars. However, when combined, these two factors—progressiveness and eco-friendliness (and Elon Musk's personal story)—have created a certain fervor. People have committed to the Tesla brand with such intensity that other car brands are no longer even options; Tesla is in a league of its own. As I mentioned earlier, it would be foolish to overlook Elon Musk's significance for the Tesla brand. He is almost a Marvel-level, lunatic genius; a controversial visionary who sees the world from a very different perspective than most people. But here also lies a problem from the perspective of Tesla's brand: when Elon Musk's personal brand is questioned, the Tesla brand is also questioned. And that's exactly what's happening right now. And as stated, Tesla's technical progressiveness is no longer so unmatched; in fact, many competitors have caught up, some have even surpassed. But what Tesla still has that is entirely unparalleled is the public's expectation of it: Tesla, surprise us! Do something that we couldn't have even imagined.

Elon Musk has been able to maintain public interest with his Space X project, but one may ask, is Tesla falling out of the spotlight? Are Teslas just becoming cars among others? Is Tesla even becoming the Toyota of electric cars, just basic fare? And it is precisely at this point that I feel that familiar itch; now would be an excellent time to find a completely new direction specifically for Tesla. And to succeed in that, we need to delve into the core of Tesla's brand.

If Tesla has wanted to revolutionize the automotive or personal transportation business, let this then also be the cornerstone of all my thinking. I started looking more closely at current business models and phenomena even loosely related to Tesla's industry. I found some kind of mental similarity from new digital platform economy businesses, for example Airbnb or Uber. They feature technical progressiveness and thorough shaking-up of a rather familiar and established industry. And since a digital interface plays a central role in many platform economy businesses, I downloaded the Tesla app on my phone. I wanted to see what kind of—perhaps even groundbreaking—features I would find. I was greatly disappointed. It felt like although Tesla's electronic interface in the car is quite progressive, the overall digital service was not very exceptional. The mobile application was purely aimed at car owners, and for those without a car, the app's task was to serve purely as a straightforward sales channel.

I pondered that since the chance for a large Tesla-non-owning audience to see the car itself is rather limited, the digital aspect could considerably expand the potential customer base. A radical idea emerged: Could Tesla's mobile app offer something so that a person who does not (yet) have a Tesla would have a reason to download Tesla's mobile application? And when I got to this thought, suddenly many things clicked into place: What if Tesla created a ride-sharing service that worked like Uber, but was entirely based on voluntariness and free of charge? It would connect people through the good old hitchhiking culture—but in a completely safe way, enabled by Tesla's mobile app.

But first I delved into the psychological dimension, and I found interesting perspectives specifically related to the fundamental pillars of the sharing economy. For instance, the most fascinating psychological aspect of Airbnb is encountering strangers. This could definitely be something that Tesla could also leverage.

I found an article about the psychological effects of encountering strangers (Van Lange 2021). In another article in *Psychology Today*, Noam Shpancer, PhD, summarizes the main points of this study:

1. Communication with strangers is psychologically safe: Strangers are far less likely to spread private information because they are unlikely to be part of one's social network.
2. Encounters with strangers can expand one's horizons. Strangers are more likely to be dissimilar in their background, attitudes, or opinions.
3. Interactions with strangers provide potential openings for various types of gains. Interactions with strangers may have

the benefit of being more likely to provide opportunities, such as suggestions or advice regarding job opportunities, a chance to learn broader skills, or a starting point for beneficial exchange or extension of one's social network.

So, my idea was that Tesla started offering a platform-economy-based transport service, where ordinary Tesla owners could offer rides through Tesla's own mobile app. And completely disruptively, this service would not be tied to any financial earning model at all. This would just be an advanced and fascinating service platform that Tesla offers—and whose function is just to create a phenomenon around Tesla and its drivers, thus acting as subtle Tesla marketing. At this stage, I have named the service tentatively as Tesla Ride. It would naturally not be a direct threat to Uber, and so I am not directly comparing Tesla Ride to Uber. The function of Tesla Ride is completely different! But what Uber has been able to prove is that such a service model can operate safely and smoothly.

It's clear why this would be an interesting service for those who do not own a car or do not have a car available at the moment they need one. But what would make Tesla drivers join the service? The psychological benefit is well justified, but I believe that Tesla drivers also need some concrete incentive. The most natural and directly beneficial incentive for drivers would be that Tesla could offer free electrical charging at their own charging stations in exchange for offered rides. I won't go into calculating or suggesting any ratios here; that's for the number crunchers. But the right direction would be that Tesla would offer free electricity, perhaps double the electricity used for the offered ride. So, an active ride provider could drive their own journeys for free.

From Tesla's perspective, Tesla Ride would have several overwhelming advantages both in terms of brand building and new car sales. I will go through some perspectives next.

Commercial Opportunity

Tesla Ride would not only be a fun, entertaining, and progressive way to offer rides and meet interesting people but also a direct way to give people the opportunity to get to know a Tesla car and ride in one. One of the most important mechanisms in car sales is test drives. Even if, in this case, the new contact doesn't get to drive the Tesla themselves, just being a passenger would expose them to Tesla's unique features, such as advanced software, acceleration, and interior. And most importantly, hearing directly from the owner about their experiences with the car. Word of mouth is proven to be the most effective form of marketing, and here it would perhaps be harnessed more systematically for marketing than ever before. Tesla's sales already occur purely through digital channels, so Tesla Ride would be a natural app-based foyer to the actual transaction.

Brand Building

Just the launch of the Tesla Ride service would immediately be one of the most talked-about PR events of the year. Tesla did it again! By expanding the use of Tesla's mobile app to include those who are not Tesla owners, Tesla would immediately multiply its potential audience compared to its current size. The image of the Tesla Ride service should be carefully constructed: It is a way for open-minded and modern people to see the world, meet new people—and move more ecologically. Research shows that most cars on the road have only the driver in them. Tesla's goal could be to change this unecological trend as well. And when the driver could charge, for example, double the electricity used during the offered ride, passengers would not feel like they are freeloading. At best, this could even form a good incentive for those living in the same neighborhood, who could easily arrange carpools to work or children's activities. But perhaps the most tantalizing use case from a storytelling perspective would be bringing together complete strangers.

Storytelling Opportunities

I am completely certain that there would be incredible opportunities for storytelling in Tesla Ride. And although traditional advertising is not Tesla's forte, there is an opportunity here to produce content for social media channels. But I'm setting the bar even higher. What if a documentary series were created to Netflix or a similar streaming service based on these rides! The fact is, when enough unknown people are matched together, certain things are bound to happen. Love stories are born. Stories emerge where a significant angel investor hops into a Tesla driven by someone with a potential business idea. Lost relatives finding each other again. Enemies burying the hatchet during a single trip. Two creative people happen to share the same car, and something completely new and surprising happens: a new movie script, an interdisciplinary exhibition idea, hit song and so on.

Perhaps Tesla Ride could also collaborate with the Carpool Karaoke show and James Corden. Using celebrities is not inherently a creative marketing idea, but in this context, it would be a natural way to generate interest in the Tesla Drive service, especially if they are offering rides to the ordinary people while doing their show.

But the one story that should kickstart all of this is the story of Elon Musk picking up an ordinary Joe. What would make it mythical is if Musk regularly, say once a month, drove some random person using Tesla Drive, and this ride would naturally be thoroughly documented. Rumors about this practice would be carefully sown into social media to ensure public attention and the creation of a phenomenon. (Addition in the spring of 2025: This idea shows how much have changed in past couple of years. This would be a true security danger to Elon nowadays.)

As with all my creative concepts, I firmly believe that the concept must be based on the human psychological driver. Tesla Drive combines many age-old human drives with current megatrends. Encountering an unknown person has always intrigued adventurers, and Tesla Drive offers a safe environment for this. The difference from Uber, for example, is that in Uber the passenger is in a financial customer relationship with the driver, so it's perfectly OK to sit quietly in the back seat. But in Tesla Drive, since the relationship between the driver and the passenger is not directly commercial, interaction is more likely to occur. One could even assume that the primary motive for both parties to use the service would be some kind of desire for interaction. And in this case, a common topic of conversation naturally emerges from the car itself. The owner's pride and the passenger's curiosity are good starting points for fruitful interaction.

I also notice here a kind of pure, good-natured spirit of old-fashioned hitchhiking. In this age, there is a strong trend of polarization, but trends also have counterforces, and in these turbulent times, the feeling of belonging is increasingly important. After all, we are of the same human species on a journey somewhere, so why not travel together?

And let's not forget the simple basic truth that social encounters, even with complete strangers, are vital to us. As the research shows, lack of social relationships is more harmful to human health than smoking, obesity, or high blood pressure! (House et al. 1988).

I think these psychological points build a strong foundation for the idea that Tesla Drive could have tremendous potential. And as stated, it would be rare for a brand to produce such a service without a direct revenue model. The aim is simply to present the brand to people and in this case also introduce the physical product. I would believe that such an interdisciplinary approach to car marketing—and at the same time creating a completely disruptive service—could be something that Elon Musk might also appreciate. Or why not some other car brand as well.

Tesla: Part II—A Framework for Brand Storytelling

OK, Tesla has hardly done any advertising. However, Tesla is already fundamentally doing things differently—changing mobility electrically, saving the planet through innovation—and this is an extremely fruitful starting point for a strong brand storytelling as well. Especially now, when there are conflicting feelings associated with Elon Musk's persona, it might be wise to point the spotlight somewhere else than him. Perhaps Tesla's corner office just hasn't been presented stories good enough?

The world is undergoing drastic changes, and sustainable solutions for the environment are being eagerly sought. I created a few stories that look at an innovation-driven business model from different angles. And as always, writing without constraints was damn fun. I also noticed that, in principle, the stories would suit many brands, but let's chalk it up to Tesla simply because they haven't ventured into brand storytelling yet. I openly admit that the following dramatizations do not adhere quite as slavishly to the ethos of conceptuality as perhaps other examples in this book. However, these stories also have at their bright core the progressiveness that I have already shown to be at the heart of Tesla's brand—and one of the strongest drivers for Tesla's customer base.

First, I wanted to write a big story about how the oil-driven world has come to the end of its road. Although only a small percentage of people belong to the psychological group of early adopters, many would like to belong. And it's this psychological feature that I'm appealing to in both stories. But the first one looks back at an era that is not exactly behind us yet but should be. I wanted to create a nostalgic atmosphere and a conceptual framework that draws a parallel between undeniably questionable phenomena of the past and fossil fuels. This way, almost subconsciously, we begin to associate negative emotions with elements that stand in the way of the green transition. Casting for this story was wonderfully easy. I chose a person for it whom I admire immensely, whose charisma is unparalleled, and who truly has perspective in life and in past decades. And even though in my own imaginary world, casting is perhaps too easy, I feel that this individual could very well join this story. I'm not just name-dropping here; I truly can see this setup in my mind.

Since Tesla will likely continue to avoid advertising in the future, I'd like to encourage readers to expand their thinking when considering potential brands. Which brands are at the forefront of the green transition? Whose target audience includes early adopters and forerunners? Feel free to use your imagination. I would really love to see this next script come to life for a Finnish company called Neste, especially if they were to restructure their business to create a new entity focused entirely on renewable fuels. This story would actually be even more relevant for them than for Tesla, as they are truly pioneers in the field of renewable fuels.

SCRIPT "Outdated World"

We are seeing Helen Mirren sitting outdoors in a stylish armchair on a wide landscape that bathes in the dramatic light of sunset.

Helen tells her story to someone we are not seeing at this point in her charming, charismatic style:

Oh, my dear! I do remember the fervor of days gone by. The thrill of premieres in the theater's dressing room, the endless parties that followed. Limousines, convertibles, the roar of engines on beach boulevards … Back then, we didn't think much, we just went and did. Blindly, like there's no tomorrow.

[The mood subtly changes, and the background music takes on darker, more dramatic tones.]
Helen continues:

But I also remember how young girls were undressed during auditions; I remember those gazes, that dirty atmosphere.

[Helen shudders as she recalls this and then continues.]

Oh, speaking of dirtiness: do you remember the smell of cig-
arette smoke? That acrid stench everywhere, clinging to your
clothes, your hair. And those toxic exhaust fumes staining the
streets, already blackened with London soot? The smog-tinted
sunsets? The smell of gasoline while refueling? Good Lord, we
were burning the remains of dinosaurs and millions-of-years-old
plants under the hoods just to move from A to B. My dear friend,
don't you think all that sounds a bit outdated now, do you?

The camera widens, and we see that in front of Helen has been a
large rusty oil pump. As Helen poses the last sentence in the form of a
personal question, the pumpjack slowly bows, as if nodding.

The payoff appears on the screen: *Fueling the Green Transition* +
Tesla logo (Figure 10).

I remember thinking back in the days that there's something oddly human about pumpjacks and their movement. Like a huge herd of creatures
nodding in the field like odd mechanical chickens. It's rather funny that a
big brand story can find its frame from such specific visual observations.

As I mentioned earlier, I also created another dramatization that fo-
cuses on the same themes but from a slightly different angle. Now the
focus is sharply on innovation and progressiveness. Few things are genuinely new in this world, but Tesla has the ability to surprise and bring
truly innovative products to the market, sometimes even somewhat cra-
zily innovative.

The next story I would have perhaps wanted to create when Steve
Jobs launched the first iPhone. However, I'm using Tesla's Cybertruck as
an example here, which by many measures brings something entirely new
to those of us who thought we'd seen it all, especially in the conservative
automotive world. But regardless, this story should not be wasted on a
product or service that doesn't genuinely bring something new to this
world—because this story happily exaggerates the concept of newness to
the stratosphere. Exaggeration is a great asset, but when you go over-
board, the product or service should be able to fulfill, in some way, the
expectations set by the story.

Figure 10 The Pumpjack

SCRIPT "Finally Something New"

We are in a white space, where a white-dressed charismatic man (like Morgan Freeman in the movie *Bruce Almighty*. Actually, why not Morgan Freeman itself!) is giving a class-made mystical cube to his child, a little girl.

The man says to the girl: "My child, you are now old enough to have your own universe."

Girl: Wow.

The girl takes the cube, and the man waves his hand above it. The magical small "big bang" takes place in the empty cube. The man sits down on a white couch, takes a book and starts to read. The girl starts to observe the cube and tells what she sees, quite fascinated.

Girl: There are tiny rocks starting to orbit the shiny ones!

Father: Uhum .... [and continues reading]

Girl: Now there's one rock having water on it ... and volcanos. The man turns the page, not lifting his eyes.

Girl: Oh, there's tiny creatures growling from the water ... wait what? Now they are starting to walk with two legs.

Girl: There are now millions of different kinds of creatures. The two-leg-ones are building houses .... Cities ... Wait, did you see that? They flew with a rocket to the other little rock!

But the father is not impressed, turning just pages of his book.

Finally, the girl says: "Ok dad, come here, this is something you really must see."

The man puts his book away and comes next to the girl, and together they are looking something very closely. Now there's a spark of enthusiasm in father's eyes and he mutters: "Interesting ..."

The camera dives into to the cube, through the millions of stars onto Earth—and finally to the Tesla plant, where the brand-new Cybertruck is gliding out from a hangar.

Voice-over: "Finally, Cybertruck is here."

Tesla logo appears on the screen (Figure 11).

Figure 11 Finally Something New

Progressive: Using Psychology to Disrupt a Generic Industry

The insurance industry is fascinating from the perspective of marketing communications, for at least two reasons. First, insurance products don't seem to have much differentiation when it comes to features—or at least, the differences are marginal. Second, there's a very strong convention in the insurance sector: They are all talking about life's tragedies and how a particular insurance company provides security. There are two contrasting approaches to this core message: deadly serious and crazy humor. I've wondered why we've seen so few approaches in between these two extremes—and this observation contains the strong assumption that there would indeed be room for something completely new. The situation is made fruitful by the fact that this is a matter of great importance to people, and thus there is naturally a place for strong and appealing storytelling.

It should also be mentioned that globally, the role of the insurance industry varies considerably depending on the country. For example, in Scandinavian welfare states, insurance is not as critical factor as, say, in the United States, where people pay market prices for basic societal services and the state doesn't subsidize these services to the same extent as in Scandinavia. But regardless, it's about securing property, health, and even life, and that evokes strong emotions.

I began to ponder the insurance world from the perspective of basic psychology. What are insurances really about? What is its ultimate benefit to a person? The basic mechanism of the business is pretty much the same as in a lottery: if people understood probability, the business would lose its foundation. 'But what if …' is the thought that works both positively behind lottery and negatively behind insuring. But let's put accidents aside for a moment and try to think about the subject from a new angle. What truths can we find? And especially truths that would have strong psychological support.

I pondered the basic driver, the motive. It's naturally about safety, the feeling of security. But I noticed that you could examine security from (at least) two different perspectives: 1. You don't have to worry when your insurances are in order. This is the industry's strongest convention. 2. The sense of security created by insurance also leads to psychological safety, which has many positive effects on a person's life. With this thought in mind, I began to dig into the research available on the subject—and found quite a bit of support for my findings. Psychological safety has been a hot trend in the corporate world in recent years. A lot of research has been done on the fact that successful teams have a psychologically safe atmosphere. However, I wanted to find scientific confirmation that psychological safety is also needed for active and positive development in a person's personal life. For example, Shannon B. Wanless's (2016) article "The Role of Psychological Safety in Human Development" strongly supports my idea. Here is a quote that sums up nicely the whole point:

> The degree to which individuals feel comfortable taking positive interpersonal risks (such as trying something new) is known as psychological safety. When individuals feel psychologically safe, they can exercise their agency to engage in experiences and interactions throughout life.

Extremely interesting was also the study, which suggests that people's creativity increases when they feel safe ("Productivity, Counterproductivity and Creativity: The Ups and Downs of Job Insecurity"). Or as neuroscientist Wendy Suzuki states in a *Forbes* interview:

> The hippocampus has been more recently implicated in creativity and imagination. Because what imagination is, is taking those things you have in your memory and putting them together in a new way. So just in the way that the hippocampus allows us to think about the past and memory, it also allows us to imagine the future. Long-term stress is literally killing the cells in your

hippocampus that contribute to the deterioration of your memory. But it's also zapping your creativity. (Probst et al. 2007)

That's it. The conceptual idea, strongly justified by psychology, can't get any clearer than this. I began to crystallize the concept into a verbal form, and arrived at the following thought:

You can do miracles when you feel safe.

It captures well the attitude I would like to see insurance companies take toward us people. It is uplifting, active, inspiring, and fundamentally one hundred percent positive. Quite soon, the idea began to feel like something clearly bigger than just a marketing communication concept— or at least it has the potential for it. This is no longer about marketing; rather, it's about an entire philosophy, ideology, and even mission.

As I mentioned earlier, the two marketing conventions in the insurance industry are either to dwell on accidents or, quite the opposite, slapstick comedy. The idea now emerging allows for more wiggle room and makes it possible to tell stories between both extremes. I also felt right away that if this concept were to take a humorous direction, there would be a much stronger insight behind it than just slapstick comedy as a superficial means of impact.

So, I found enough research data to validate this perspective. I was almost overwhelmed by the wealth of approaches I could take. But from a brand perspective, the situation is fruitful: such strong psychological insight ensure that the brand has material for its marketing for years to come. The basic idea of my entire book is to illustrate my thinking with concrete marketing examples. I chose the insurance company Progressive as my example brand, as it has shown the ability and willingness to do impactful brand storytelling. Naturally, it's also beneficial that Progressive aligns well with the brand philosophy I created, both in name and in the values behind that name.

Initially, I started creating dramatizations whose basic idea is that when a person has basic security in place, they can take new courageous steps in their lives, create something new, and perhaps even something socially significant. I wanted to build an approach that is inspiring and encouraging. On the other hand, I was also aware that lofty ideas often lead to pompous dramatizations. I absolutely wanted to bring in some lightness, humor, and even a little absurdity. So, I started exaggerating boldly and searching for rather extreme stories. I wanted to show that in moments crucial to humanity, it has always been about the courage to take new steps into the unknown. I was amused by the idea of bringing a modern insurance company into historical events in an absurd way and as if appropriating the historical event, in this case, for the Progressive brand.

BRAND FILM "Explorer"

We are in fifteenth century, and we are seeing the great ship *Santa María* in a harbor ready to departure. Next, we are on the ship's command bridge where the helmsman is asking Columbus rather worried: "*Ma se la Terra fosse piatta?*" (Subtitles: But what if the Earth is flat?)

COLUMBUS: [with great confidence] *Calmati. Ho un Progressive Travel Insurance.* (Subtitles: Calm down, I have Progressive Travel Insurance.)

Text on the screen: You can do miracles when you feel safe. + Progressive logo (Figure 12).

BRAND FILM "Wheel"

We are seeing a beautiful wide landscape and a quite high hill in the middle of scene. Some active volcanos in the background. There's two tiny characters on the top of the hill. We are cutting closer to them, and we are seeing two cavemen with their fur clothes on. The other one has crafted a huge wheel from a stone. He's laying himself on the inner circle of the wheel and asking his pal: "*Gro urgh argho!*" (Subtitles: All right, give me a push!)

The other one a bit skeptically looking the downhill: "*Naa grih ghuuko?*" (Subtitles: Are You really sure?)

The man inside the wheel says with calming tone: "*Ar hugh ko grah Progressive Car Insurance.*" Subtitles: (No worries, I have Progressive Car Insurance.)

Text on the screen: You can do miracles when you feel safe. + Progressive logo

Figure 12 Columbus

BRAND FILM "Garage"

We are in the 1970s suburban and we are seeing a house and garage from the bird's-eye view. Camera is slowly approaching the garage from outside.

We are cutting inside seeing two slightly hippie looking guys (reminding surprisingly young Steve Jobs and Steve Wozniak). They are staring at a retro style self-made computer. Wozniak look-alike is biting an apple and putting it on the top of the computer so everyone understands what we are referring to.

WOZNIAK: Are you really sure about this?

JOBS: No worries, we have Progressive Business Insurance.

Text on the screen: You can do miracles when you feel safe. + Progressive logo

BRAND FILM "Small Step"

We are seeing a spaceship that has landed on the Moon. We cut inside the spaceship. Two astronauts with their spacesuits on are standing in front of the closed front door. They are keeping their helmets in their arms.

One of the astronauts is casually, totally stress-free practicing his famous line: "That's one small step for a man ...."

The other one is nodding toward the door and asking slightly worried: "Are you sure about this ...?"

FIRST ONE: Calm down, we have Progressive insurance.

Text on the screen: You can do miracles when you feel safe. + Progressive logo (Figure 13).

Figure 13 The Moon

Brand Behavior

Because the psychological underpinning is so strong, I see tremendous potential in this concept from a brand behavior perspective. We could, for example, create a TV show where people could discuss their uncertainties and dreams—along with an expert to identify the reasons that prevent those dreams from being fulfilled. People's lives would be followed after uncertainty factors had been minimized and decisive steps toward dreams had been taken. The whole idea of the program would be to validate the brand philosophy of the main sponsor, Progressive, that "You can do miracles when you feel safe." It would be incredibly great if the brand could genuinely help people make crucial decisions in their lives. For instance, a couple who have long dreamed of trying to have a child but have hesitated for financial or health reasons. People's stories and destinies can be sourced quite broadly, and even those stories not directly tied to a Progressive insurance product can be included. We believe in the truth that when an insurance company improves someone's overall sense of security, decisions in all aspects of life become easier.

In line with its brand philosophy, Progressive could also sponsor innovative start-ups or young entrepreneurs. On an individual level, it would be in line with the concept to establish a scholarship program for promising students—and thus help them achieve their dreams and move closer to their ideal selves. Brand actions and behavior are fertile from a marketing perspective because they have much more evidentiary power than mere advertising—but on the other hand, brand actions can easily also provide content for traditional advertising channels.

In this concept, I particularly believe in its perfect feasibility and psychologically flawless insight. The verbal distillation may be somewhat long, but it aligns well with, say, Snickers' "You are not you when you are hungry." Indeed, the brand promise can be over that magical three words if the message requires it. Above all, this brand philosophy requires the promise "You can do miracles when you feel safe" to be systematically and consistently repeated. It's like a mantra that strengthens with repetition.

Electrify America: Changing Weakness into a Winning Brand Concept

Since I started this book during the pandemic, many phenomena and hidden social structures revealed by pandemic were on my mind. It is, of course, clear that a good and long-lasting marketing communications concept cannot rely on an exceptional period, but interestingly the pandemic helped us see things in a new light. I also found researched information on the effects of the pandemic. Dr. Asanka Gunasekara from Swinburne University crystallized the outcomes of their research (2022):

> Our recent research shows that people have re-evaluated what they want out of work and life. Overwhelmingly, they want to work less. Before the pandemic, half of our survey participants described themselves as 'work-centric'. After the pandemic, most of these participants switched to classify themselves as 'family-centric' or 'self-centric', which means they are more focused on family time, leisure, and other personal pursuits.

I started pondering the fundamental reasons for this change. In my opinion, we have seen work, at least traditional office work or expert work, surprisingly unchanging for decades. The pandemic revealed that office work is, at least in part, an outdated construct that took shape after World War II. Indeed, the rigid hierarchy and stiff organizational structure were built directly on military principles. We have subtly become accustomed to this way of working, but office work has not been able to respond to the needs of a changing world due to its militarylike lack of flexibility. This gap has made people feel unwell and increased general dissatisfaction. The pandemic was a crisis that forced us into new ways of operating but also offered an opportunity to adapt these operating models to better meet people's needs, even in expert or white-collar work.

But I wanted to delve even deeper into the effects of the pandemic. What did the pandemic force us to do? Over time, an idea began to take shape in my mind, and I also reflected it against Asanka Gunasekara's research: For example, where does the shift from work-centricity to family-centricity stem from? I concluded the following: the fundamental impact of the pandemic on people, both individually and throughout society, was to stop. We were forced to pause, both physically and mentally. This pause made people think about their lives, their desires, their potential, and how to utilize that potential from a new perspective. People had mostly been following established paths in their lives, but when forced to pause, they began to consider how to utilize their potential in a way that would bring in their life as much happiness as possible. We were forced to stop, and from that followed—or at least could follow—something good. I latched onto this theme of stopping and began to look for information on the benefits and significance of smaller or larger pauses in life, as I already sensed the possibilities for a strong marketing communication concept.

It's not exactly news that taking breaks during a busy day improves performance, helps with focus, and enhances creativity. I also found an extremely interesting study in which Hans Henrik Sievertsen, PhD, with his colleagues investigated the significance of breaks on test performance among students in a Danish school (2016):

> In Denmark, as in many other places across the globe, test time is determined by the weekly class schedule and computer availability at schools. We find that, for every hour later in the day, test scores decrease by 0.9% SDs. In addition, a 20- to 30-minute break improves average test scores. Importantly, a break causes an improvement in test scores that is larger than the hourly deterioration … A break causes an improvement in test score that corresponds to about 1,900 USD higher household income, almost 2 months of parental education, or 19 school days.

A 30-minute break leads to an improvement in test scores equivalent to 19 school days of studying! In my opinion, the benefit ratio is significant.

I also found an interesting study where William S. Helton, PhD, a professor of human factors and applied cognition at George Mason University, examined students' ability to perform a concentration-demanding task that lasted 45 minutes (Rees et al. 2017). Some of the group performed the task without breaks, while others took a five-minute break halfway through, during which they used various relaxation methods. Every group that took a break performed better in the task than those who did it continuously. Helton describes the situation as follows: "We don't know exactly what in the brain gets depleted, but when you do a cognitively demanding task, it operates as though there's a 'mental fuel' that gets burned up."

Next, I started pondering which brand could have a strong foundation for an exceptional marketing communication concept. And I couldn't think of anything sensible. Somehow, all imaginable approaches seemed to easily veer into the realm of the pretentious. And while I believe in profound psychological insights, one can't—and often shouldn't—dive too deeply. Storytelling can have a profound layer without unnecessary seriousness. Intuitively, I felt that something other than a serious or educational approach would fit; I just had to find the perfect match. And once again, I was in a fortunate position in that there was no tight deadline. I got to let the idea mature in peace. Then, serendipity intervened. At the time, we still had a gasoline car, but I had quietly decided that the next one would be electric. I actively followed the discussion about electric cars, and perhaps the hottest topic in electric driving was, and still is, car charging, charging times, and the accessibility of charging stations. And then it hit me: we have an industry centered around making people to stop! The potential brand could be a traditional gas station or a modern electric charging brand. Coincidentally, William S. Helton's quote about "mental fuel" concealed a great seed of a big brand concept?

After this realization, the rest was considerably easier. The conceptual approach formed in my mind like this: Pausing in life is proven to be beneficial and even a trend. A humorous and utterly undeniable marketing communication concept, for example for North America's largest electric car charging company Electrify America, would own this positive pausing theme and say that Electrify America is unquestionably the master of these life's micro-pauses! The concept would provide a hilarious, but logically flawless approach that could be tapped into endlessly. I was also tickled by the setup where a generally negative thing (waiting to car charging) is turned into something positive with great confidence. Such a brazen approach is fertile ground for creating communication that will almost inevitably attract attention. And at best, it tickles those with a sense of humor; the grumps can get indignant all they want.

Too often, companies cultivate obvious statements at the core of their marketing. For example, service stations might tout clichéd thoughts like

"Keeps You Moving" or "Takes You Further" or something similar. No shit Sherlock! Every single person knows why you have to stop at a service station. You don't need to teach or even communicate that to people. The concept I created would offer a fresh and new perspective on a familiar subject—thereby creating a strong foundation for distinct and memorable marketing communication. And making Electrify America a slightly more interesting brand than its competitors.

I condensed the concept into the verbal form "Pause in Life." The sentence itself is not surprising or insightful, but when combined with a service station brand, something completely new is born—and hopefully memorably crazy.

I wrote several film script dramatizations, where I specifically wanted to use humor. The first is a manifesto, where I wanted to create an absurd contrast between the events visible in the picture and the lofty manifesto speech. The story still follows a classic formula with a twist at the end.

BRAND FILM "Pause in Life"

A beautiful evening is getting dark; the sun has just set. At first, we see only a parked modern electric car with foggy windows, rocking presumably in some parking lot. The camera pulls back slightly and reveals a David Attenborough look-alike (or the real one, if he would agree to appear in the advertisement). He crouches in front of the car and whispers to the camera with great intensity:

> Motion is an incredibly fascinating thing. When a butterfly wing flutters, there's always a microscopic pause at the ending point of the motion. Music consists of notes, but in fact, between each note, there's a microscopic pause. Before the Big Bang, there was a moment of perfect stillness.

David continues:

> Although motion is, of course, a basic prerequisite for life ...

> [At this point, the camera moves closer to the back of the car and reveals the charging cable plugged in. The camera follows

the cable to the Electrify America charging station, which becomes the final image of the advertisement.]

... pausing and stopping are also essential for life and its continuation.

The text appears over the image: *Pause in Life* + Electrify America logo (Figure 14).

Figure 14 The Art of a Pause

I saw a lot of potential in this humorous story. It's both a somewhat crazy manifesto and, on the other hand, a brand story in a classically concise advertising format. Each of us has surely seen more than enough overly long manifesto films, where stock footage illustrates a voice-over that mainly drones on with lofty brand storytelling suited for an annual report. In my opinion, that entire genre should be criminalized.

But I thirsted for more. What other brand stories could be told from this insight? And this is where I want to say that I've too often encountered a creative team that is no longer willing to stretch their thinking in new directions, but rather gets stuck in one approach. On the other hand, I understand that since the time of creative professionals is money, it may not necessarily make sense to do creative work just for the joy of creating. But my situation was different. If someone does Sudoku to keep their brain sharp, this book project serves as good mental exercise for me. So, I continued to develop the concept "Pause in Life." I believed in a structure where the benefits of pausing in life are discussed loftily—only to ultimately reveal that we equate stopping to charge with the lofty act of pausing in life. I also wanted to maintain a certain absurd atmosphere. And so, another story was born.

BRAND FILM "CEO"

We are in a beautiful corner office with a scenic view. Behind his desk in front of a large window sits Electrify America's CEO Robert Barrosa, who is speaking intensely to the camera: "Pausing in life is proven to be beneficial. And we are helping people discover this skill."

The camera zooms out and we see a magnificent butterfly flying outside the window. Robert points to the butterfly, which comes to a halt as if frozen in mid-air. Robert continues: "When you pause, you can see the beauty in things …."

Robert accidentally knocks a full cup of coffee off the edge of the table but snaps his fingers to stop the cup in mid-air, grabs the mug, and picks the frozen coffee droplets back into the mug—then places the mug back on the table: "On the other hand, by pausing, you can avoid wrong turns and many discomforts."

Robert rises from behind his desk and walks over to the window while speaking, looking out: "We believe that if the world needs anything, it's pausing."

Down in the parking lot, two cars have backed into adjacent charging stations. A man and a woman plug cables into their own cars. Their eyes meet, shift shyly away, and then lock onto each other. A small smile lights up on both of their faces. We are back in the office; Robert continues clearly excited to the camera: "Did you see? The art of pausing."

+ Electrify America logo and payoff "Pause in Life" appears on the screen.

Short but Effective

I was delighted to find the Robert Barrosa at the center of brand storytelling. Around a good character, various other approaches can easily emerge, one of which could produce short dramatizations for digital channels, for example.

SCRIPT "Art of Pausing"

We see a close-up of an old "sacred" book, on the cover of which are gold-embedded letters spelling "The Art of Pausing." The camera zooms out, and we see that the book is in the hands of a dreadlocked guru. The guru is sitting in a loincloth, in the lotus position, on top of some sort of pole, although we can't see what kind of pole it is. The guru lifts his gaze from the book and speaks directly to the camera: "The benefits of pausing in life are undeniable. For example: better concentration, reduced stress, increased creativity ...."

The camera zooms out, and we see that the guru is sitting on top of an Electrify America futuristic charging station. The camera widens further, and we see Robert Barrosa standing next to the charging station. Robert plugs the charging cable into his car and continues imitating the guru's serene tone with a twinkle in his eyes: "... and that by pausing, you go further in life."

The message *"Pause in Life"* appears on the screen + Electrify America logo

Brand Behavior

Because the concept "Pause in Life" is based on physical action, an actual pause, it also provides quite good conditions for various brand behavior initiatives. One of the most obvious would be to encourage people to utilize the time spent charging their cars—and Electrify America could document these productions. If the reward were, say, free lifetime charging, Electrify America's social media channels could be buzzing. Interestingly enough, there is a real meta-level to this concept in this book, as I have written several pages while my car has been charging!

Another thought: we could hire a well-known musician who would write the songs for their upcoming album during charging times, Ed Sheeran comes to mind without trying. It's nice to be able to name-drop without any reservations. Or why not some popular detective novelist could write a book while charging. The idea behind all these actions is to prove that stopping at an Electrify America charging station is not just a waste of time but can also be used beneficially.

What if we are building a few flagship charging stations, which would be accompanied by stylish meditation rooms? At best, there could be staff brewing green tea, playing meditative music, or even teaching the basics of meditation. Naturally, there can't be too many of these flagships; their purpose is to attract attention, garner earned media and generate interest on social media—and to manifest the concept *Pause in Life*.

KitKat: Brand Concept as a Coping Mechanism

This is one of the most recent additions to this book. Let it serve as a small snack (pun intended) alongside the slightly more substantial chapters. The idea for this chapter largely stemmed from three different factors.

First, while delving into Electrify America, I explored the theme of taking a break in depth, making the subject thoroughly familiar to me.

Second, I have recently been studying Mark Ritson's insights, and he rightfully cites KitKat as a strong brand. KitKat has spent decades consistently reinforcing the same brand philosophy and even the same advertising approach—people taking a break from their busy lives to enjoy a KitKat. Some readers may recall that I referenced Ritson at the very beginning of this book, saying that he is right about almost everything. However, as I have followed his lectures, one thought has continued to bother me: KitKat's marketing communications are fairly mediocre—perhaps even dull. I found some genuinely funny ads from a decades ago, but the more recent ones are bland and filled with clichéd advertising humor. While I firmly believe in systematically brand building and maintaining long-term consistency in storytelling, I realized that KitKat is not fully leveraging the potential of its brand philosophy by sticking solely to the same narrow theme: Life is hectic, take a break—illustrated by showing exhausted office workers. There is nothing inherently wrong with this message, and I'm not saying it should be abandoned entirely, but I had an insight: with a slight shift in perspective, KitKat could become a far more meaningful brand without losing its core identity and tone of voice.

The third factor was the fact that, during the process of writing this book, the world has only continued to grow stranger—and not always in a positive way. I already touched on polarization and troubling societal trends in the Virgin Atlantic section, so I won't go deeper into that here. But it's undeniable that absurd phenomena, famous characters, and events have become increasingly prevalent in our daily news cycles. We are bombarded with an overwhelming amount of information, news, and even historical upheavals—at some point, we all need a break from it all. And KitKat could be the brand that, in a way that aligns with its humorous brand personality, simply says: "Enough. I need a break from all of this." And just like that, their brand concept fits this idea perfectly. So I began thinking about a phrasing that would preserve the idea of the iconic brand concept's slogan, but could work, for example, as a headline-level statement—and it felt quite given to end up at the following thought: *Give me a break!*

While this approach immediately felt quite natural, I wanted to find some scientific support for my thinking and evaluate the business potential. How much anxiety has increased in recent years? How many people feel overwhelmed by the turmoil in the world? The trend was strikingly clear. For example, the American Psychiatric Association's annual mental health poll shows that U.S. adults are feeling increasingly anxious. In 2024, 43 percent of adults reported feeling more anxious than they did the previous year, up from 37 percent in 2023 and 32 percent in 2022.

Most of us have likely experienced this trend firsthand in recent times. This led to the idea that KitKat could address this global climate in its own way—through sarcastic humor—encouraging people to take a well-deserved break from it all. And naturally, KitKat is perfectly positioned to offer that break. Humor has also been scientifically proven to be an excellent way to cope with stressful situations and alleviate anxiety. I came across an interesting study on prisoners of war from the Vietnam War era (Henman 2001). In this study they found out, that the repatriated Vietnam prisoners of war are suffering almost no mental illness, and the effective use of humor seems to be one of the reasons for their health. The literature by and about prisoners of war from several recent wars indicates prisoners often found humor to be an effective coping mechanism, a way of fighting back and taking control. By defining humor as an element of communication and by thinking of resilience as a communication phenomenon, the links between humor and resilience become more apparent. I find this profoundly humane. The harder the times, the more people turn to humor to survive! I've read that even in tightly controlled dictatorships—where joking about the dictator or those in power could cost you your life—people still make jokes about them. There's something truly striking about that! And yes, I found it as absurd as you might feel to read a study about Vietnam War POWs while writing a chapter about KitKat, but that's how it can be when seeking psychological support for one's thinking.

This resurgence of humor is also evident in the world of marketing. Humor is a rising trend because people are craving something a little lighter in these times. And from a brand's perspective, what could be better than making people chuckle, even just a little? But unlike the countless funny examples we see in Super Bowl commercials, KitKat could take a slightly more sarcastic approach—after all, what else can we do but laugh at the state of the world? We wouldn't just be comedians making jokes purely for entertainment or mechanically trying to amuse people. Instead, we would offer a way for people to process the phenomena of our time through the humorous lens that KitKat's brand provides. The following film script illustrates hopefully my point.

SCRIPT "Give Me a Break!"

We see a relaxed man in his 30s sitting on his living room couch. He picks up the remote and turns on the TV. A news broadcast is on, and the news anchor announces: "Breaking news: Scientists have just successfully crossbred a dolphin and a giraffe …."

The man raises his eyebrows and switches the channel. Another news broadcast is playing, with the anchor reporting: "The President has proposed a project to Congress to purchase the Great Wall of China and relocate it to the southern border…."

The man sighs and changes the channel again, only to find yet another news broadcast: "A strange strain of bird flu is now spreading rapidly across the globe. Symptoms include an urge to crow at dawn and a strong desire to build nests in trees …." (We might even see news clips of people behaving strangely: strutting like roosters with rapid head moves and crowing.)

The man scoffs in disbelief, exclaiming, "Give me a break!" Somewhat unexpectedly, the news anchor seems to hear the man's sigh, picks up a KitKat bar, and tosses it out of the TV screen straight to the man, who catches it. The man unwraps the KitKat bar and snaps off a piece. Leaning back, a satisfied smile spreads across his face.

The logo and tagline appear on the screen: Have a Break ... Have a KitKat.

It was incredibly easy—and in some way even therapeutic—to come up with humorously absurd "news" that still felt close to reality. It's a proven fact that humor is an excellent way to process even the most difficult topics, and KitKat would have a golden opportunity to tap into this survival mechanism. Not too seriously but rooted in a real insight. I believe this perspective could inspire an entire series of content that comments on current phenomena in a slightly absurd way. And what's best (or perhaps worst), this era seems to be a better scriptwriter than any creative mind, constantly feeding the Give me a break idea with endless flow of initiatives. All KitKat needs to do is stay alert and respond to the phenomena it sees fit.

Brand Behavior

I indulged for a moment in the idea of KitKat becoming an active social media brand, finding the weirdest, most over-the-top, and most extreme Internet absurdities, and simply commenting, "Give me a break!" This phrase, paired with the instantly recognizable KitKat brand in the profile picture, would make the comment completely clear. Of course, KitKat could also continue and spark the conversation by emphasizing the importance of taking a break in this chaotic world—with a healthy dose of humor and sarcasm, naturally.

What would be the ultimate outcome if KitKat started behaving this way? Just like my example with Virgin Atlantic, in this case, too, people could begin using the brand as a direct statement. For instance, by putting a KitKat bumper sticker on their car, they could signal that they've had enough of the current state of the world. I admit this isn't an easy goal to achieve, but for example by enlisting the right influencers to actively use KitKat and the phrase "Give me a break!" in social media discussions, the phenomenon could take off.

Well then, I feel like I've told enough stories. It has been fun and rewarding. And remember, the ideas, concepts, and dramatizations presented in this book can easily be scaled or adapted to many other brands besides the ones I've chosen here as examples. Many of the brands that ended up as examples have been selected for specific reasons that I've explained. However, many of the structures I've developed are based more on industry-specific truths. Are the ideas I've presented then useless because they have already been published in this book? I don't believe, even in my wildest dreams, that this book will be read by anything more than a very small circle of people in the marketing field. That's a handful among the world's population. The brands have millions of people in their commercial target groups. For these millions or hundreds of millions, the ideas and stories presented in this book can only become familiar through the brands. Thank you for sticking with me this far—let's stay in touch!

References

Ahona Guha, D. Psych. 2021. "Are You Your Own Worst Enemy?" *Psychology Today*. https://www.psychologytoday.com/ca/blog/of-prisons-and-pathos/202105/are-you-your-own-worst-enemy.

Bluerock, Grace. 2023. "The 9 Most Common Regrets People Have at the End of Life." https://www.mindbodygreen.com/articles/the-most-common-regrets-people-have-at-the-end-of-life?srsltid=AfmBOorCRn4rDSqNg7stVs0RuDe4A1igzYUFxL7AiQqNsQ8rbTp8eZIi

Cao, J., A.D. Galinsky, and W.W. Maddux. 2013. "Does Travel Broaden the Mind? Breadth of Foreign Experiences Increases Generalized Trust." https://journals.sagepub.com/doi/abs/10.1177/1948550613514456

Davidai, Shai, and Thomas Gilovich. 2018. "The Ideal Road Not Taken: The Self-Discrepancies Involved in People's Most Enduring Regrets." *Emotion* (Washington, D.C.) 18(3):439–52. Doi:10.1037/emo0000326.

Gilovich, T., and V.H. Medvec. 1994. "The Temporal Pattern to the Experience of Regret." *Journal of Personality and Social Psychology* 67 (3): 357–65.

Gorzelitz, J., B. Trabert, H.A. Katki, S.C. Moore, E.L. Watts, and C.E. Matthews. 2022. "Independent and Joint Associations of Weightlifting and Aerobic Activity with All-Cause, Cardiovascular Disease and Cancer Mortality in the Prostate, Lung, Colorectal and Ovarian Cancer Screening Trial." *British Journal of Sports Medicine* 56:1277–83.

Gunasekara, Asanka N., Melissa A. Wheeler, and Anne Bardoel. 2022. "The Impact of Working from Home during COVID-19 on Time Allocation across Competing Demands." *Sustainability* 14 (15): 9126.

Henman, Linda D. 2001. "Humor as a Coping Mechanism: Lessons from POWs." *Humor Research* 14 (1): 83–94.

House, J.S., K.R. Landis, and D. Umberson. 1988. "Social Relationships and Health." *Science* 241 (4865): 540–5.

Lieberman, Daniel E. July/August 2015. "Is Exercise Really Medicine? An Evolutionary Perspective." *Current Sports Medicine Reports* 14 (4): 313–19.

Probst, T. M., S. Stewart, M. L. Gruys, and B. W. Tierney. 2007. "Productivity, Counterproductivity and Creativity: The Ups and Downs of Job Insecurity." *Journal of Occupational and Organizational Psychology* 80:479–97. Doi:10.1348/096317906X159103.

Rees, A., M.W. Wiggins, W.S. Helton, T. Loveday, and D. O'Hare. 2017. "The Impact of Breaks on Sustained Attention in a Simulated, Semi-Automated Train Control Task." *Applied Cognitive Psychology* 31:351–9.

Sievertsen, H.H., F. Gino, and M. Piovesan. 2016. "Cognitive Fatigue Influences Students' Performance on Standardized Tests." *Proceedings of the National Academy of Sciences of the United States of America* 113(10):2621–4. Doi:10.1073/pnas.1516947113

Van Lange, P. A. M., and S. Columbus. 2021. "Vitamin S: Why Is Social Contact, Even with Strangers, So Important to Well-Being?" *Current Directions in Psychological Science* 30(3):267–73.

Wanless, S.B. 2016. "The Role of Psychological Safety in Human Development." *Research in Human Development* 13 (1): 6–14.

About the Author

Juuso Kalliala is a seasoned marketing communications professional with over 20 years of experience. He built a long career as a copywriter in various advertising agencies in Finland, including international network agencies such as BBDO Helsinki, Wunderman Thompson, and TBWA Helsinki. During his years in advertising agencies, he operated through his own company, Mind Tattoo Storytelling. For the past five years, he has served as a creative lead at one of the Finland's largest company, S Group. He is a passionate brand storyteller who enjoys all kinds of narratives. A dedicated reader, he immerses himself in literature daily, primarily fiction. Lately, like so many others, he has been concerned about the polarization of the world and the troubling developments for humanity, even in Western democracies.

Index

* 9 7 8 1 6 3 7 4 2 9 0 0 6 *